Join the latest Tokyo street fashion craze!

Stylish Remakes

Upcycle Your Old T's, Sweats and Flannels
into Trendy Street Fashion Pieces

Violette Room

TUTTLE Publishing

Tokyo | Rutland, Vermont | Singapore

Contents

T-SHIRTS

01

Embellished Bow T-shirt

before

how to make it → **p.34**

02

Dress with Lace Skirt

before

how to make it → **p.37**

03
Long Tank Top

before

TRUST
ME

+

how to make it → **p.39**

04

Cat T-shirt

before

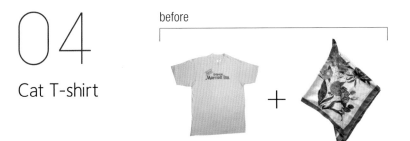

how to make it → **p.41**

05

All-In-One Shorts

before

+

+

how to make it → **p.44**

06

Children's Romper

before

how to make it → **p.48**

07

Half-and-Half Dress

before

how to make it → **p.52**

Flannel Shirts

08

Jacket with Gathered Waist

before

how to make it → **p.55**

09

Big Bow Blouse

before

how to make it → **p.57**

10

Coat Dress

before

+

how to make it → **p.60**

11

Half-and-Half Skirt

before

+

how to make it → **p.62**

Borders

12

Stripes and Liberty Print Dress

before

how to make it → **p.64**

13

Cardigan with Detachable Collar

before

how to make it → **p.66**

14

Tunic from an
Oversized Scarf

before

+

how to make it → **p.70**

15

Pouch

before

how to make it → **p.71**

College Sweats

16

Animal Print Collar Top

before

how to make it → **p.75**

17

Tube Top Dress

before

how to make it → **p.77**

18

Half-and-Half
Big Tunic

before

how to make it → **p.80**

19

Hoodie Dress

before

how to make it → **p.82**

Gabardine Coats

20

Coat with Scarf Collar and Details

before

 +

how to make it → **p.84**

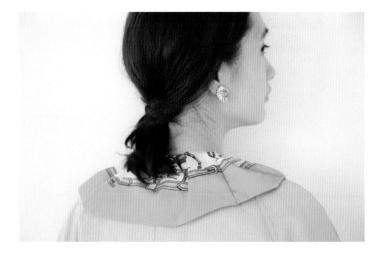

21

Scarf Motif Charms

before

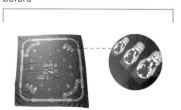

how to make it → **p.86**

22
Trench Coat
Poncho

before

+

how to make it → **p.87**

Bandannas

23

Patchwork Dress

before

how to make it → **p.89**

24

Child's Camisole
and Skirt

before

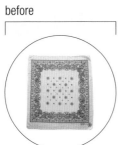

how to make it → **p.91**

Drawstring Purse

before

how to make it → **p.94**

Let's Upcycle!

These inventive projects are constructed from recycled printed or striped T-shirts, flannel shirts, college sweatshirts, jackets, trench coats and bandannas. Thrift store men's items make up the bulk of the source material, but women's items are included as well. We've included tips on how to select garments that can be upcycled and we've made sure to feature items you will easily find at most thrift stores.

Measurements are given in imperial units as well as metrics. All imperial measurements are approximate. We have attempted to conform to as closely as possible to standard imperial fabric, elastic and ribbon widths, as well as to button and snap diameters. Please don't worry if the materials available to you don't conform to these measurements exactly.

Look!

When sewing with stretchy materials like knit jersey and interlock that T-shirts and sweatshirts are typically made of, it's important to use ball-point needles and thread specifically designed for knit fabrics. This is to prevent thread breakage and other challenges that come with sewing knits. Stretching the fabric in the direction you are sewing is also key for secure stitches.

Regular stitch

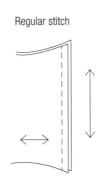

Stretch fabric
as you sew

Overlock or zig zag stitches

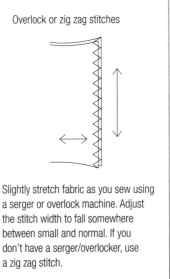

Slightly stretch fabric as you sew using a serger or overlock machine. Adjust the stitch width to fall somewhere between small and normal. If you don't have a serger/overlocker, use a zig zag stitch.

01 Embellished Bow T-shirt

▷ page 06

The rolled up sleeves give this T-shirt a casual and sassy feel. Create a quilted effect by filling the bow with synthetic or cotton stuffing and randomly stitching on the surface of the bow. No need for perfection here! Have fun positioning the bow to balance out any pre-existing prints or designs.

[FINISHED MEASUREMENTS]
(Based on Men's size L)
Length 26 in (66cm)   Bust 42 in (106cm)

＊Measurements are strictly for reference and actual measurements will depend on the T-shirt utilized.

[MATERIALS/SUPPLIES]
T-shirt
Fabric for bow, as needed (in this case, the scraps from a flannel shirt remake were used)
Synthetic or cotton stuffing, enough to fill the bow

＊How to choose a T-shirt
Choose whatever size appeals to you, from snug to oversized. Add whimsy with printed T's that include people or animal designs.

[PREPARATION]
①Place the bow pattern piece directly on the front of the T-shirt and determine the overall balance and design you'd like. Modify the position and length of the pattern piece as you see fit.
②Trace the modified pattern pieces onto the scrap fabric. We will refer to these pieces as the bow pieces.

before

[How to make]

① Machine stitch the left and right bow tail (or end) pieces to the T-shirt and gently fill with stuffing. Repeat with the left and right top portions of the bow.

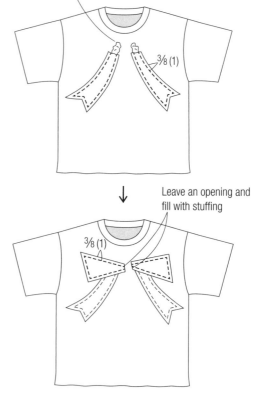

Using an awl or thin stick, distribute the stuffing evenly within the end pieces.

⅜ (1)

Leave an opening and fill with stuffing

⅜ (1)

② Stitch the center of the bow, making sure to leave an opening for the stuffing. Fill with stuffing, then stitch closed.

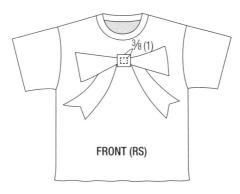

③ Cut bodice length and/or sleeves to desired length. Then fold up the sleeve two or three times, and hand sew every few inches around the rolled sleeve to hold in place.

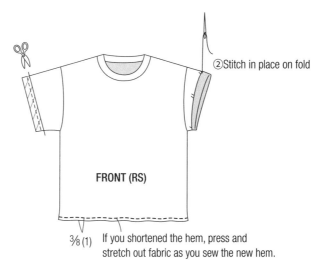

②Stitch in place on fold

FRONT (RS)

³⁄₈ (1) If you shortened the hem, press and stretch out fabric as you sew the new hem.

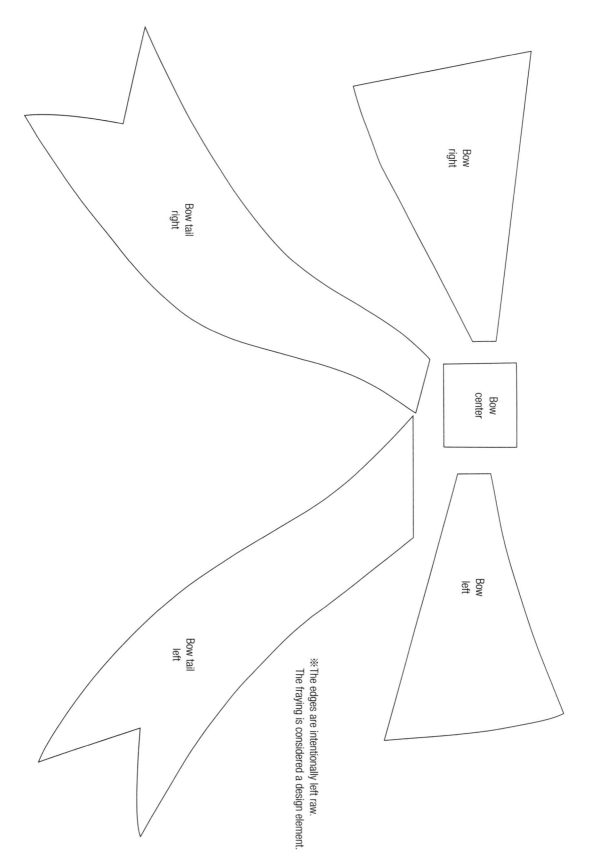

Bow
right

Bow tail
right

Bow
center

Bow
left

Bow tail
left

※The edges are intentionally left raw.
The fraying is considered a design element.

02 Dress with Lace Skirt

▷ page 07

Snip the sleeves and tweak the top and skirt, and you have a one-of-a-kind outfit in no time. The key is to combine the tough band T-shirt vibe with the delicate lace, balancing the hard with the soft.

[FINISHED MEASUREMENTS]
(Based on Men's size M)
Dress length 45 in (110cm)   Bust 37 in (92cm)

∗ Measurements are strictly for reference and actual measurements will depend on the T-shirt utilized.

[MATERIALS/SUPPLIES]
T-shirt
Lace (for skirt) 1½ yd (1.3m) at 52 in (130cm) wide
Lining (for skirt) 1⅜yd (1.2m) at 48 in (122cm) wide

∗ How to choose a T-shirt
Look for slightly oversized, faded men's T's with edgy rock or punk band logos and prints.

before

[How to make]

① Cut the sleeves to a French sleeve length.

② Baste sleeve openings.

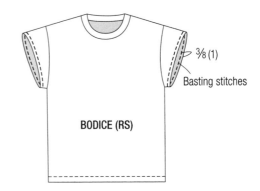

⅜ (1)

Basting stitches

BODICE (RS)

③ Sew the side seams of skirt, right sides facing. Repeat with lining.

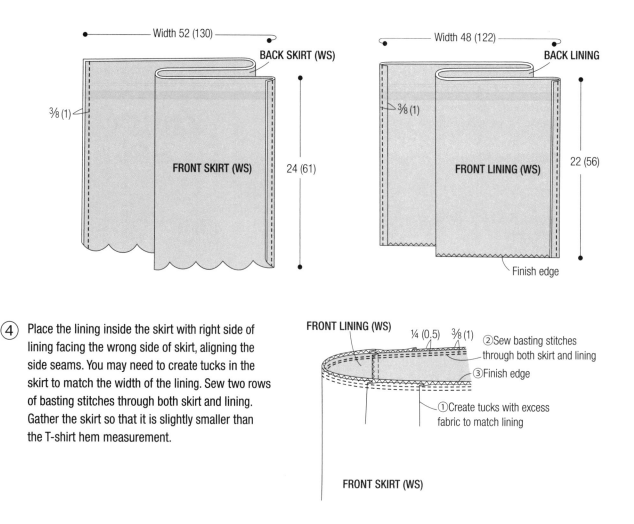

④ Place the lining inside the skirt with right side of lining facing the wrong side of skirt, aligning the side seams. You may need to create tucks in the skirt to match the width of the lining. Sew two rows of basting stitches through both skirt and lining. Gather the skirt so that it is slightly smaller than the T-shirt hem measurement.

⑤ Look at the general balance and proportion of the T-shirt with the skirt, and adjust the length of the T-shirt accordingly. Fold up excess length of the T-shirt toward wrong side. Align the upper edge of the skirt with the top of the folded edge of the T-shirt, right sides facing. Baste the skirt to T-shirt to hold in place. Then top stitch from right side.

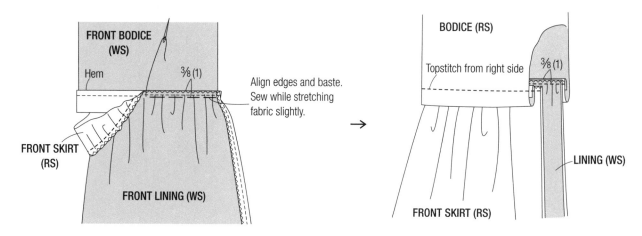

03 Long Tank Top

▷ page 08

A stylish combo showcasing a T-shirt's existing print with a pop of color. The extra length makes this an easy-to-wear wardrobe staple.

[FINISHED MEASUREMENTS]
(Based on Men's size S)
Length 29 in (73cm)   Bust 33 in (84cm)

∗Measurements are strictly for reference and actual measurements will depend on original shirts utilized.

[MATERIALS/SUPPLIES]
Tank top
T-shirt

∗How to choose a tank top and T-shirt
Look for a T-shirt that is about the same size or slightly larger than the tank top. Fitted or a bit loose works nicely for this garment. This is a great design for playing up whimsical prints and pastel colors.

before

+

TRUST ME

[How to make]

① Cut along tank top cutting line as shown.

Use top portion only

Cut the front bodice into a curved sweetheart neckline

Cutting line

FRONT (RS)   1⅝ (4)   BACK (RS)   1⅝ (4)

1⅜ (3.5)

¼ (0.5)

Cut the back in a straight line

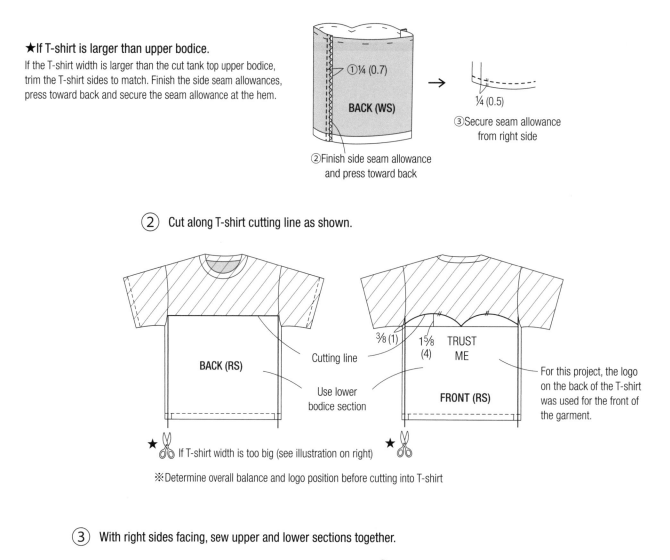

★If T-shirt is larger than upper bodice.

If the T-shirt width is larger than the cut tank top upper bodice, trim the T-shirt sides to match. Finish the side seam allowances, press toward back and secure the seam allowance at the hem.

① ¼ (0.7)

BACK (WS)

→

¼ (0.5)

③Secure seam allowance from right side

②Finish side seam allowance and press toward back

② Cut along T-shirt cutting line as shown.

BACK (RS)

Cutting line

Use lower bodice section

⅜ (1) 1⅝ (4) TRUST ME

FRONT (RS)

For this project, the logo on the back of the T-shirt was used for the front of the garment.

★ ✂ If T-shirt width is too big (see illustration on right) ★ ✂

※Determine overall balance and logo position before cutting into T-shirt

③ With right sides facing, sew upper and lower sections together.

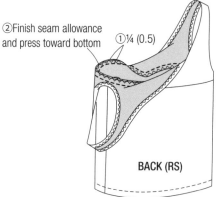

②Finish seam allowance and press toward bottom ① ¼ (0.5)

BACK (RS)

04 Cat T-shirt

▷ page 09

Cut off the neckband and hem, roll up the sleeves and add a cat appliqué made out of a scarf. Leave the hem raw to give it a curled edge. Try to use the section of a scarf with an interesting, eye-catching print. Depending on your mood, try stitching a charming expression on the cat's face.

[FINISHED MEASUREMENTS]
(Based on Men's size M)
Length 22 in (56cm)   Bust 38 in (96cm)

∗Measurements are strictly for reference and actual measurements will depend on the T-shirt utilized.

[MATERIALS/SUPPLIES]
T-shirt
Scarf
Interfacing as needed
Embroidery floss, size 25, 6 ply (Brown, Cream)
   as needed

∗How to choose a T-shirt
Let your preference shine here, whether you like a close or looser fit. Simple, plain T's are recommended to allow the cat to stand out. Add an element of sweetness with pastel hues.

[PREPARATION]
Cut out the cat pattern piece and place directly on the T-shirt to gauge the overall proportion. Adjust the size and position to your liking. Ironing the fusible interfacing onto the scarf before tracing and cutting the cat pattern will make the job easier.

before

[How to make]

① Trace the cat pattern onto the right side of the scarf. Include facial features except the whiskers. Using embroidery floss, hand stitch along the traced lines.

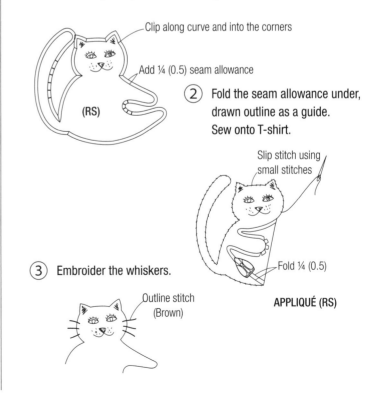

Clip along curve and into the corners

Add ¼ (0.5) seam allowance

(RS)

② Fold the seam allowance under, drawn outline as a guide. Sew onto T-shirt.

Slip stitch using small stitches

Fold ¼ (0.5)

APPLIQUÉ (RS)

③ Embroider the whiskers.

Outline stitch (Brown)

④ Cut the ribbed neckband from about ⅜ in (1cm) above the seam. If the hem and sleeves look too long, cut to desired length.

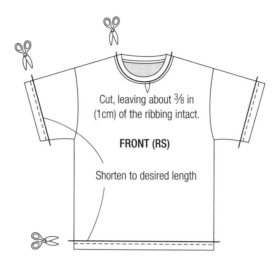

Cut, leaving about ⅜ in (1cm) of the ribbing intact.

FRONT (RS)

Shorten to desired length

⑤ Baste hem. Roll up the sleeves two or three times and stitch in several places to hold in place. Leave the neckband raw, and stretch it out for a casual, relaxed look.

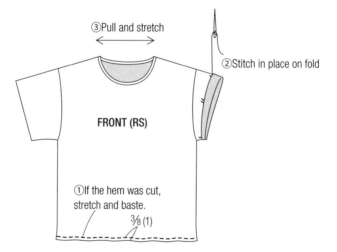

③Pull and stretch

②Stitch in place on fold

FRONT (RS)

①If the hem was cut, stretch and baste.

⅜ (1)

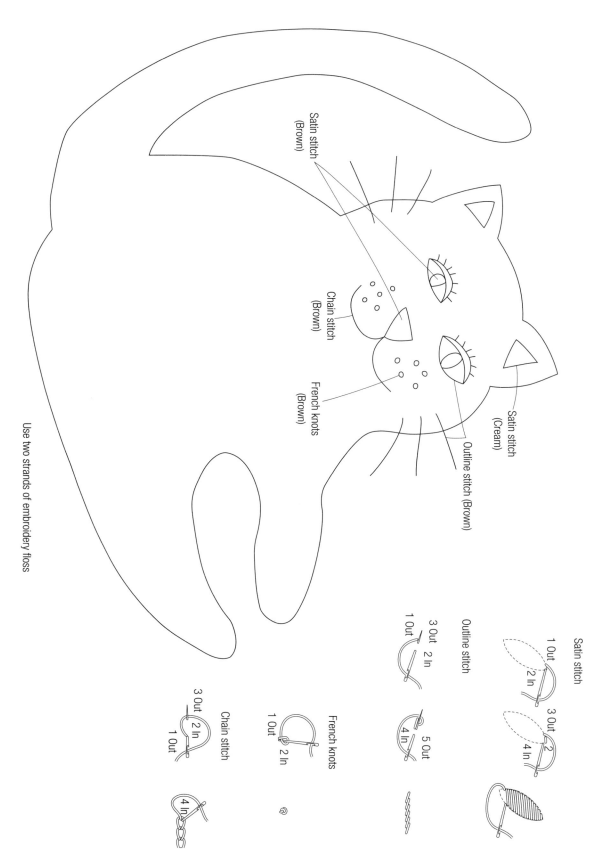

Satin stitch (Brown)

Chain stitch (Brown)

French knots (Brown)

Satin stitch (Cream)

Outline stitch (Brown)

Use two strands of embroidery floss

Satin stitch

1 Out 2 In 3 Out 4 In

Outline stitch

3 Out 2 In 1 Out

French knots

1 Out 2 In

Chain stitch

3 Out 2 In 1 Out 4 In

05 All-In-One Shorts

▷ page 10

For this unique outfit, two T-shirts are converted into a pair of shorts, which are then docked to a tank top to create an "all-in-one" garment. Depending on the fit of the tank top, you can vary the general look and feel. Make sure to select a roomy tank top if you want an overall relaxed outfit.

[FINISHED MEASUREMENTS]
(Based on Men's size S for all garments)
Length 41 in (105cm)   Bust 29¼ in (74cm)
Hip 33 in (84cm)

＊Measurements are strictly for reference and actual measurements will depend on original garments utilized.

[MATERIALS/SUPPLIES]
Tank top
T-shirt (for shorts) x 2
Snaps x 2 sets at ⅜ in (1cm) diameter

＊How to choose the tank top and T-shirts
Depending on your preference, go slim-fitting or loose. When selecting T-shirts to create the shorts, keep in mind the desired fit. Look for garments that have faded, vintage appeal.

[PREPARATION]
Draft the shorts pattern based on the reference diagram

before

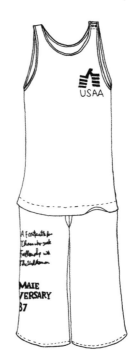

[How to make]

Shorts reference diagram

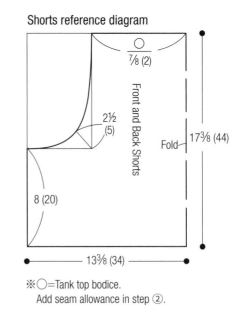

※◯=Tank top bodice.
　Add seam allowance in step ②.

① Cut apart the tank top shoulder seams.
Cut the two T-shirts into a rectangular shape.

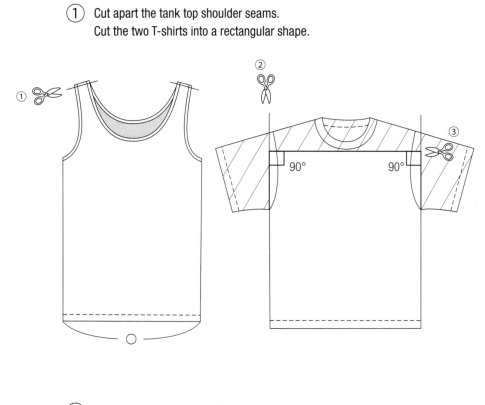

② Draft shorts, tank top shoulder placket and facing.
Try to incorporate any existing prints/designs into the pattern pieces.

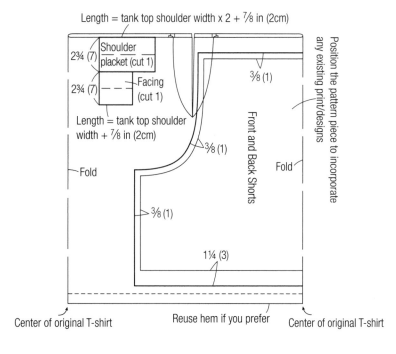

Length = tank top shoulder width x 2 + 7/8 in (2cm)

2¾ (7) — Shoulder placket (cut 1)

2¾ (7) — Facing (cut 1)

Length = tank top shoulder width + 7/8 in (2cm)

Fold

3/8 (1)

3/8 (1)

3/8 (1)

1¼ (3)

Front and Back Shorts

Position the pattern piece to incorporate any existing print/designs

Fold

Center of original T-shirt

Reuse hem if you prefer

Center of original T-shirt

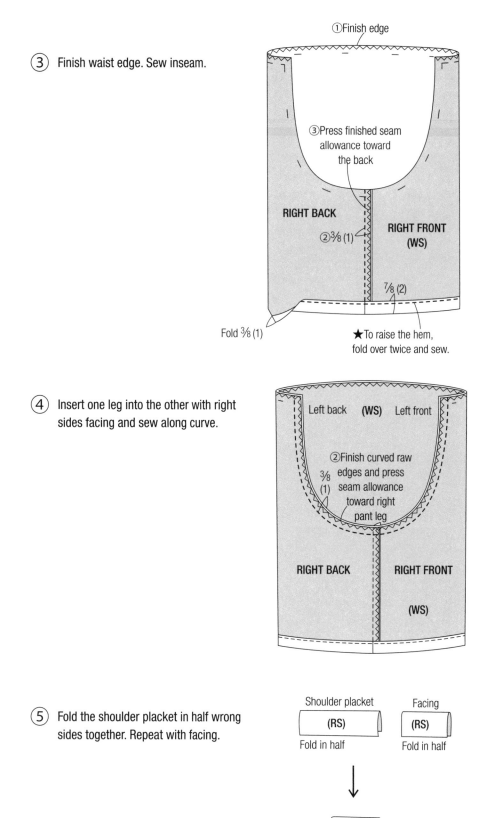

③ Finish waist edge. Sew inseam.

①Finish edge

③Press finished seam
allowance toward
the back

RIGHT BACK

RIGHT FRONT
(WS)

②⅜ (1)

⅞ (2)

Fold ⅜ (1)

★To raise the hem,
fold over twice and sew.

④ Insert one leg into the other with right
sides facing and sew along curve.

Left back   (WS)   Left front

②Finish curved raw
edges and press
seam allowance
toward right
pant leg

⅜
(1)

RIGHT BACK   RIGHT FRONT

(WS)

⑤ Fold the shoulder placket in half wrong
sides together. Repeat with facing.

Shoulder placket

(RS)

Fold in half

Facing

(RS)

Fold in half

(RS)

Fold in half again, then sew along
edge and turn right side out.

(6) Sew tank top shoulder seams. On the left shoulder, attach shoulder placket on the right side and facing on wrong side, then sew right shoulder.

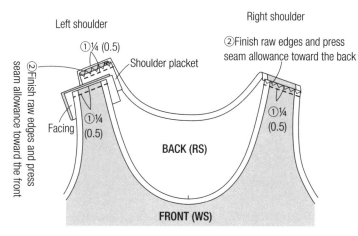

Left shoulder

Right shoulder

①¼ (0.5)

Shoulder placket

②Finish raw edges and press seam allowance toward the back

②Finish raw edges and press seam allowance toward the front

Facing

①¼ (0.5)

①¼ (0.5)

BACK (RS)

FRONT (WS)

(7) Attach snaps to shoulder placket and facing.

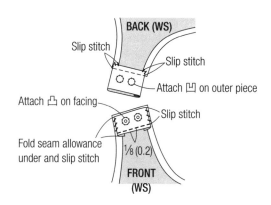

BACK (WS)

Slip stitch

Slip stitch

Attach 凹 on outer piece

Attach 凸 on facing

Slip stitch

Fold seam allowance under and slip stitch

⅛ (0.2)

FRONT (WS)

(8) Fold and press the hem of the tank top toward the wrong side, then align shorts on top with right sides together. Baste, making sure stitches are sewn through all layers.

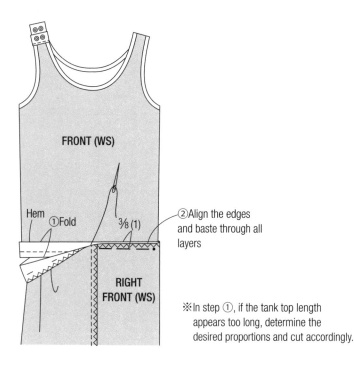

FRONT (WS)

Hem ①Fold

⅜ (1)

②Align the edges and baste through all layers

RIGHT FRONT (WS)

※In step ①, if the tank top length appears too long, determine the desired proportions and cut accordingly.

(9) Stretch the fabric as you sew from the front, making sure to prevent shifting.

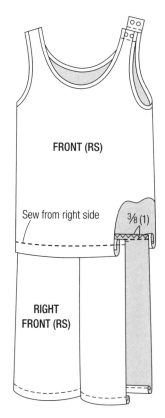

FRONT (RS)

Sew from right side

⅜ (1)

RIGHT FRONT (RS)

06 Children's Romper
▷ page 11

A kid-friendly, knee-length rompers adorned with ruffled sleeves. Using comfortably worn T-shirts will feel extra soft against the delicate skin of children.

[FINISHED MEASUREMENTS]
31½–35½ in (80–90cm)
Length 18½ in (46.5cm)   Bust 20½ in (52cm)

[MATERIALS/SUPPLIES]
T-shirt
Snaps x 5 sets of ⅜ in (1cm) diameter
          1 set of ¼ in (0.7cm) diameter

＊How to choose T-shirt
For ease of construction, select women's small-sized T's. It might take a bit of digging, but search for vintage pop designs for an extra dose of cuteness.

[PREPARATION]
Draft the pattern piece using the reference diagram.

before

Drafting

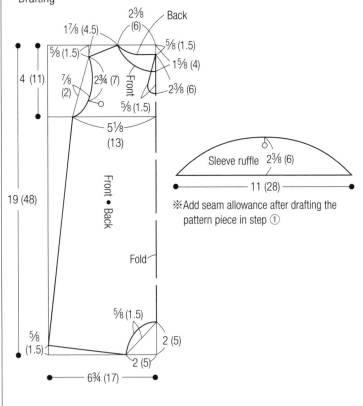

Sleeve ruffle 2⅜ (6)
11 (28)

※Add seam allowance after drafting the pattern piece in step ①

[How to make]

(1) Before drafting the pattern pieces, cut off the T-shirt sleeves, then cut front and back of shirt apart at the side seams.

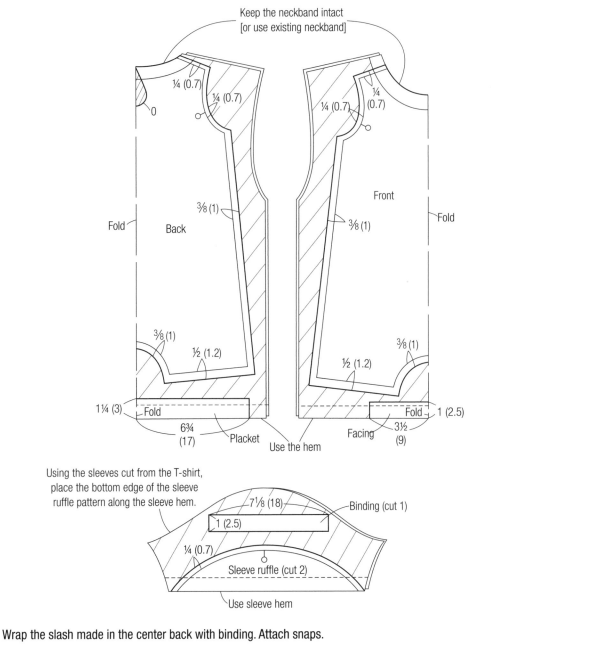

Keep the neckband intact
[or use existing neckband]

¼ (0.7)

¼ (0.7)

0

¼ (0.7)

¼ (0.7)

¼ (0.7)

Front

Fold   Back

⅜ (1)

⅜ (1)

Fold

⅜ (1)

½ (1.2)

⅜ (1)

½ (1.2)

⅜ (1)

1¼ (3)   Fold

6¾
(17)   Placket

Use the hem

Facing

Fold   1 (2.5)

3½
(9)

Using the sleeves cut from the T-shirt,
place the bottom edge of the sleeve
ruffle pattern along the sleeve hem.

7⅛ (18)   Binding (cut 1)

1 (2.5)

¼ (0.7)

Sleeve ruffle (cut 2)

Use sleeve hem

(2) Wrap the slash made in the center back with binding. Attach snaps.

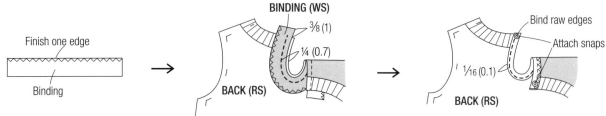

Finish one edge

Binding

BINDING (WS)

⅜ (1)

¼ (0.7)

BACK (RS)

Bind raw edges

Attach snaps

1/16 (0.1)

BACK (RS)

③ Gather sleeve ruffles, pulling threads to form a 5½ in (14cm) width.

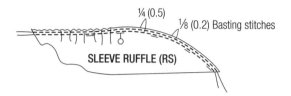

¼ (0.5) ⅛ (0.2) Basting stitches

SLEEVE RUFFLE (RS)

④ Sew shoulder seams together. Baste sleeve ruffles where marked around armhole.

①Sew shoulder seams and finish seam allowances. Press seam allowances toward back.

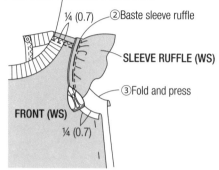

¼ (0.7) ②Baste sleeve ruffle

SLEEVE RUFFLE (WS)

③Fold and press

FRONT (WS)

¼ (0.7)

⑤ Attach sleeve ruffles.

②Finish seam allowance. Press toward bodice.

SLEEVE RUFFLE (WS)

①

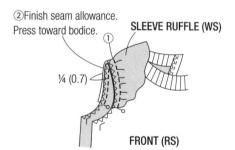

¼ (0.7)

FRONT (RS)

⑥ Sew side seams, then stitch the armhole seam allowance in place, and then sew hem.

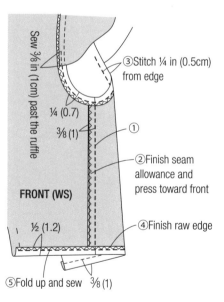

Sew ⅜ in (1cm) past the ruffle

③Stitch ¼ in (0.5cm) from edge

¼ (0.7)

⅜ (1) ①

②Finish seam allowance and press toward front

FRONT (WS)

④Finish raw edge

½ (1.2)

⑤Fold up and sew ⅜ (1)

(7) Attach facing.

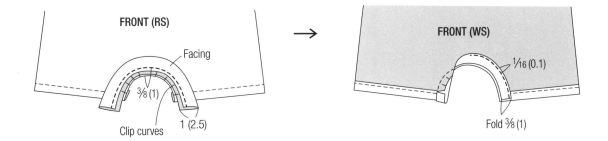

FRONT (RS)

Facing

3/8 (1)

Clip curves

1 (2.5)

FRONT (WS)

1/16 (0.1)

Fold 3/8 (1)

(8) Create snap placket and attach to the back piece.

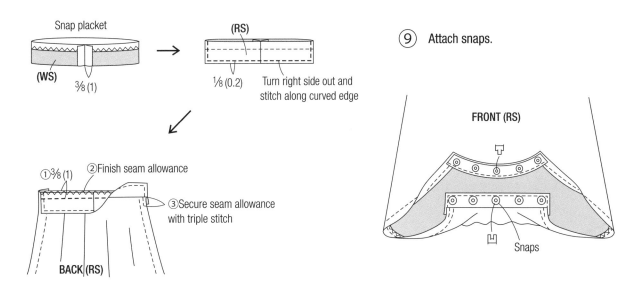

Snap placket

(WS)

3/8 (1)

(RS)

1/8 (0.2)

Turn right side out and
stitch along curved edge

① 3/8 (1)

②Finish seam allowance

③Secure seam allowance
with triple stitch

BACK (RS)

(9) Attach snaps.

FRONT (RS)

Snaps

07 Half-and-Half Dress

▷ page 12

What makes this dress stand out is the pairing of two different patterns and color schemes. You can have a lot of fun looking for complementary combos, and the shape of the shirt shines in this dress, with clever details like two large pockets made from the sleeve openings.

[FINISHED MEASUREMENTS]
(Based on Men's size L)
Length 36½ in (93cm)   Bust 44 in (112cm)

∗Measurements are strictly for reference and actual measurements will depend on original flannel shirt utilized.

[MATERIALS/SUPPLIES]
Flannel shirts (preferably of the same size) x 2

∗How to choose flannel shirts
Here, vintage looks were selected. Keep in mind that if the shirts are too small, the length may not be adequate. Try to find larger men's sizes and select prints that work well together.

before

[How to make]

① Place the two shirts (we'll call them A and B) back-to-back and cut sleeves.
The longer pieces of cut sleeves will become the shoulder straps; cut off the cuffs.
Try to err on the longer side for the shoulder strap pieces.

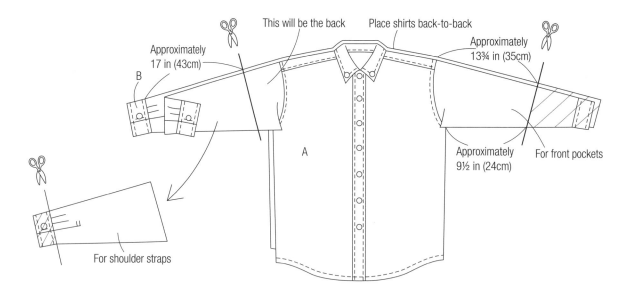

Approximately 17 in (43cm)

This will be the back

Place shirts back-to-back

Approximately 13¾ in (35cm)

B

Approximately 9½ in (24cm)

For front pockets

A

For shoulder straps

② Take one of the cut-off sleeves to form a pocket. Close each end using French seams. Repeat with other sleeve/pocket.

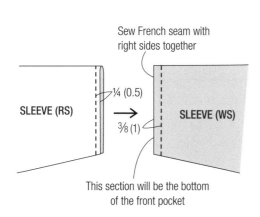

Sew French seam with right sides together

SLEEVE (RS)

¼ (0.5)

⅜ (1)

SLEEVE (WS)

This section will be the bottom of the front pocket

③ Taking one side of each shirt, button them together. If the buttons and buttonholes do not align, adjust the button positions.

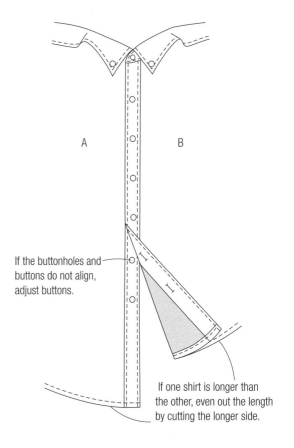

A

B

If the buttonholes and buttons do not align, adjust buttons.

If one shirt is longer than the other, even out the length by cutting the longer side.

④ Using the cut-off sleeve pieces, create shoulder straps. Adjust the length of the straps based on your preference.

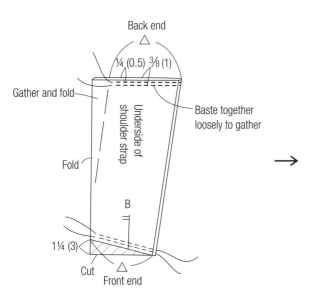

Back end

¼ (0.5) ⅜ (1)

Gather and fold

Underside of shoulder strap

Baste together loosely to gather

Fold

B

1¼ (3)

Cut

Front end

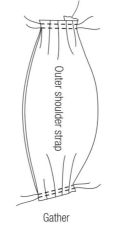

Fold toward underside of shoulder strap

Outer shoulder strap

Gather

5 Attach shoulder straps to bodice.

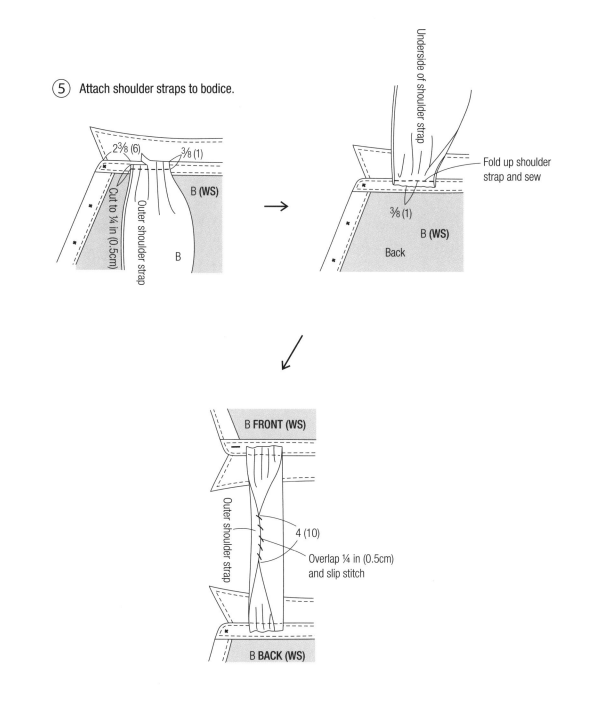

2⅜ (6)   ⅜ (1)

Cut to ¼ in (0.5cm)

Outer shoulder strap

B (WS)

B

Underside of shoulder strap

Fold up shoulder strap and sew

⅜ (1)

B (WS)

Back

B FRONT (WS)

Outer shoulder strap

4 (10)

Overlap ¼ in (0.5cm) and slip stitch

B BACK (WS)

08 Jacket with Gathered Waist

▷ page 14

Simply by modifying a men's flannel shirt with a cinched waist and puffed, three-quarter sleeves, you can create a jacket with a distinctly feminine look.

[FINISHED MEASUREMENTS]
(Based on Men's size M)
Length 21½ in (54cm)   Bust 37½ in (95cm)

∗ Measurements are strictly for reference and actual measurements will depend on original flannel shirt utilized.

[MATERIALS/SUPPLIES]
Flannel shirt
Elastic—29½ in (75cm) at 1½ in (4cm) wide

∗ How to choose a flannel shirt
Seek out larger men's sizes with a classic color combination.

before

[How to make]

① Cut off sleeves and hem, remove stitches from the cut-edge of cuffs.

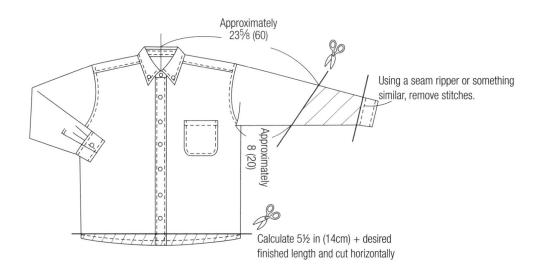

Approximately 23⅝ (60)

Using a seam ripper or something similar, remove stitches.

Approximately 8 (20)

Calculate 5½ in (14cm) + desired finished length and cut horizontally

(2) Gather sleeves (use illustration as reference) to fit the sleeve cuff.

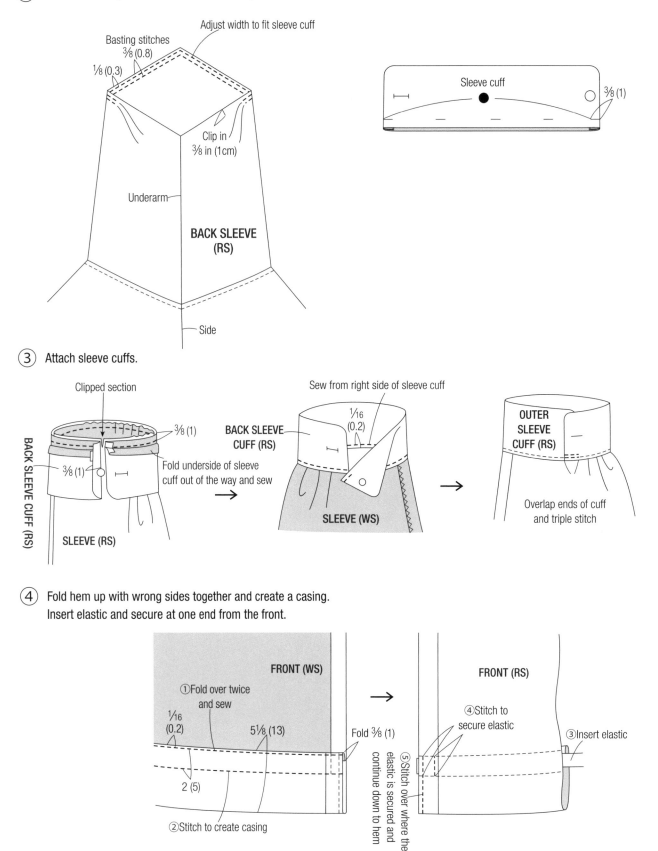

Adjust width to fit sleeve cuff

Basting stitches
3/8 (0.8)

1/8 (0.3)

Clip in
3/8 in (1cm)

Underarm

BACK SLEEVE
(RS)

Side

Sleeve cuff

3/8 (1)

(3) Attach sleeve cuffs.

Clipped section

BACK SLEEVE CUFF (RS)

3/8 (1)

3/8 (1)

Fold underside of sleeve
cuff out of the way and sew

SLEEVE (RS)

Sew from right side of sleeve cuff

BACK SLEEVE
CUFF (RS)

1/16
(0.2)

SLEEVE (WS)

OUTER
SLEEVE
CUFF (RS)

Overlap ends of cuff
and triple stitch

(4) Fold hem up with wrong sides together and create a casing.
Insert elastic and secure at one end from the front.

FRONT (WS)

①Fold over twice
and sew

1/16
(0.2)

5 1/8 (13)

Fold 3/8 (1)

2 (5)

②Stitch to create casing

FRONT (RS)

④Stitch to
secure elastic

③Insert elastic

⑤Stitch over where the
elastic is secured and
continue down to hem

09 Big Bow Blouse
▷ page 15

For this top, the original collar and top two buttons
are removed (though the collar stand remains)
to create lapels. The cut sleeves and collar portions
are then repurposed to create a playful big bow,
which is actually a brooch that can be detached.

[FINISHED MEASUREMENTS]
(Based on Men's size L)
Length 25½ in (65cm)   Bust 42 in (106cm)

＊Measurements are strictly for reference and actual
measurements will depend on original flannel shirt utilized.

[MATERIALS/SUPPLIES]
Flannel Shirt
Brooch pin back

＊How to choose a flannel shirt
We used a shirt with a nostalgic feel, and we recommend
a close-fitting size for optimal balance.

before

[How to make]

(1) Cut the sleeves, bodice and collar as specified.

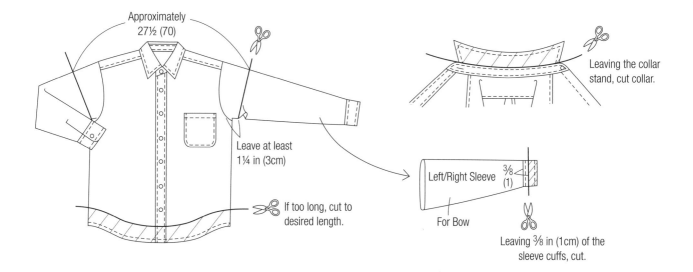

Approximately
27½ (70)

Leave at least
1¼ in (3cm)

If too long, cut to
desired length.

Leaving the collar
stand, cut collar.

Left/Right Sleeve   3/8
(1)

For Bow

Leaving 3/8 in (1cm) of the
sleeve cuffs, cut.

② Remove the top two buttons. Determine how much you want to fold open, then stitch lapels to bodice.

③ Fold over sleeve edge twice and sew. If the sleeve opening is too wide, overlap the sleeve under the arm and stitch.

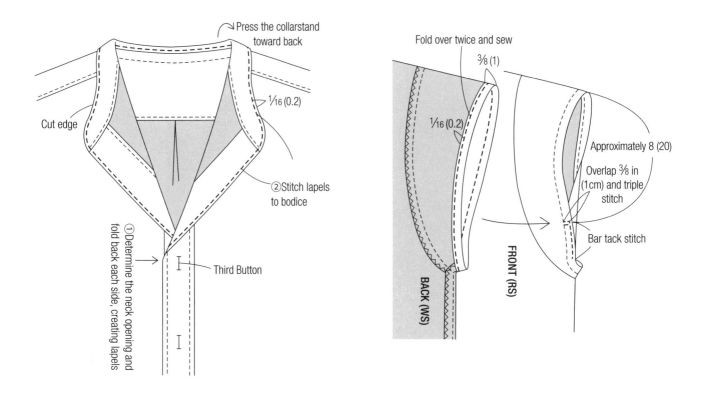

Press the collarstand toward back

Cut edge

1/16 (0.2)

②Stitch lapels to bodice

①Determine the neck opening and fold back each side, creating lapels

Third Button

Fold over twice and sew

3/8 (1)

1/16 (0.2)

BACK (WS)

FRONT (RS)

Approximately 8 (20)

Overlap 3/8 in (1cm) and triple stitch

Bar tack stitch

④ If you shortened the length, fold over edge twice and hem.

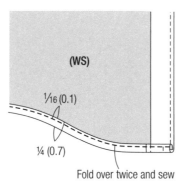

(WS)

1/16 (0.1)

1/4 (0.7)

Fold over twice and sew

⑤ Make the bow with the cut-off collar and left and right sleeves. Attach brooch pin back.

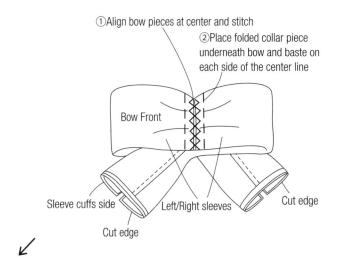

①Align bow pieces at center and stitch

②Place folded collar piece underneath bow and baste on each side of the center line

Bow Front

Sleeve cuffs side

Cut edge

Left/Right sleeves

Cut edge

Cut edge

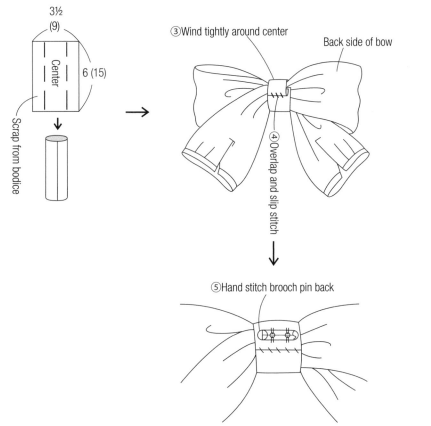

3½
(9)

Center

6 (15)

Scrap from bodice

③Wind tightly around center

Back side of bow

④Overlap and slip stitch

⑤Hand stitch brooch pin back

10 Coat Dress

▷ page 16

Tie in the front as a dress or tie at the back to wear as a coat or cardi…such a versatile piece of clothing for your wardrobe! Get creative with pattern mixing for a variety of looks. Adjust the ease to fit (it looks best when it's not oversized).

[FINISHED MEASUREMENTS]
(Based on Men's size XL)
Length 37½ in (95cm)   Bust 45½ in (116cm)

∗ Measurements are strictly for reference and actual measurements will depend on original flannel shirt utilized.

[MATERIALS/SUPPLIES]
Flannel Shirts (preferably of the same size) x 2

∗ How to choose flannel shirts
We used shirts with a vintage feel, and we recommend a close-fitting size for optimal balance.

before

[How to make]

① Cut apart each shirt. For one shirt (we'll call it A), the top portion will be used and for the other shirt (B), the lower portion will be used. For shirt B, cut off the collar up to but not including the collar stand. Also cut off the sleeves.
The seam allowance of the front yoke for shirt B will be used, so remove the stitches.

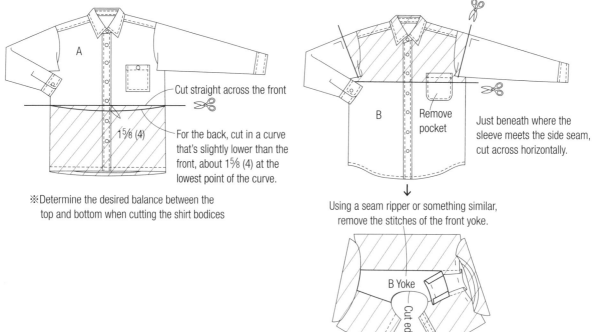

A

Cut straight across the front

1⅝ (4)

For the back, cut in a curve that's slightly lower than the front, about 1⅝ (4) at the lowest point of the curve.

※Determine the desired balance between the top and bottom when cutting the shirt bodices

B

Remove pocket

Just beneath where the sleeve meets the side seam, cut across horizontally.

↓

Using a seam ripper or something similar, remove the stitches of the front yoke.

B Yoke

Cut edge

---

② Lay wrong side of yoke B on top of right side of yoke A.
Fold yoke B under to match yoke A's shape and baste.

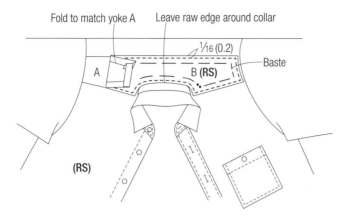

③ Attach shirts A and B at waist using a French seam (press seam allowance toward A).

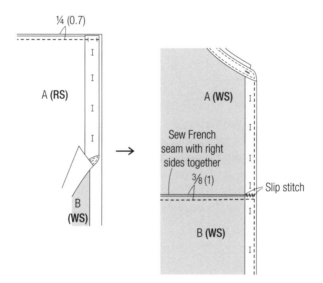

④ Attach sleeves from shirt B to bodice.

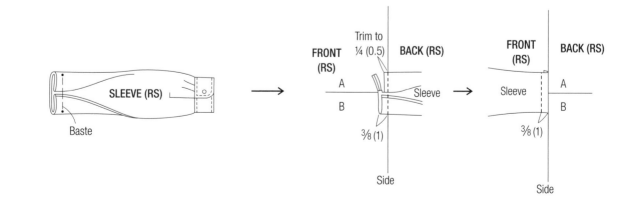

11 Half-and-Half Skirt

▷ page 17

More half-and-half fun, this time in skirt form! Hunt down larger sized flannel shirts to allow for ample length—you'll be cutting them to hit just above the knee. The shirt sleeves are transformed into pockets and the ingenious design makes it look as though another shirt is tied around the waist.

[FINISHED MEASUREMENTS]
(Based on Men's size M)
Waist 26½ in (68cm)   Skirt Length 21½ in (55cm)

∗ Measurements are strictly for reference and actual measurements will depend on original flannel shirt utilized.

[MATERIALS/SUPPLIES]
Flannel shirts (preferably of the same size) x 2

∗ How to choose flannel shirts
We used shirts in classic plaids, and we recommend a close-fitting size for optimal balance.

before

+

[How to make]

① Place shirts (we'll call them A and B) back-to-back and cut off sleeves and bodice as specified.

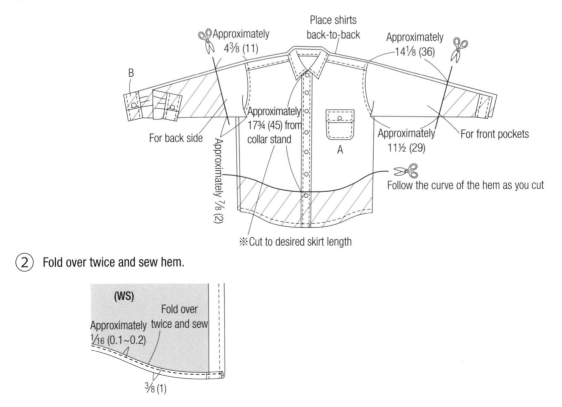

Approximately 4⅜ (11)

Place shirts back-to-back

Approximately 14⅛ (36)

B

For back side

Approximately 17¾ (45) from collar stand

Approximately ⅞ (2)

A

Approximately 11½ (29)

For front pockets

Follow the curve of the hem as you cut

※Cut to desired skirt length

② Fold over twice and sew hem.

(WS)

Fold over twice and sew

Approximately 1/16 (0.1~0.2)

⅜ (1)

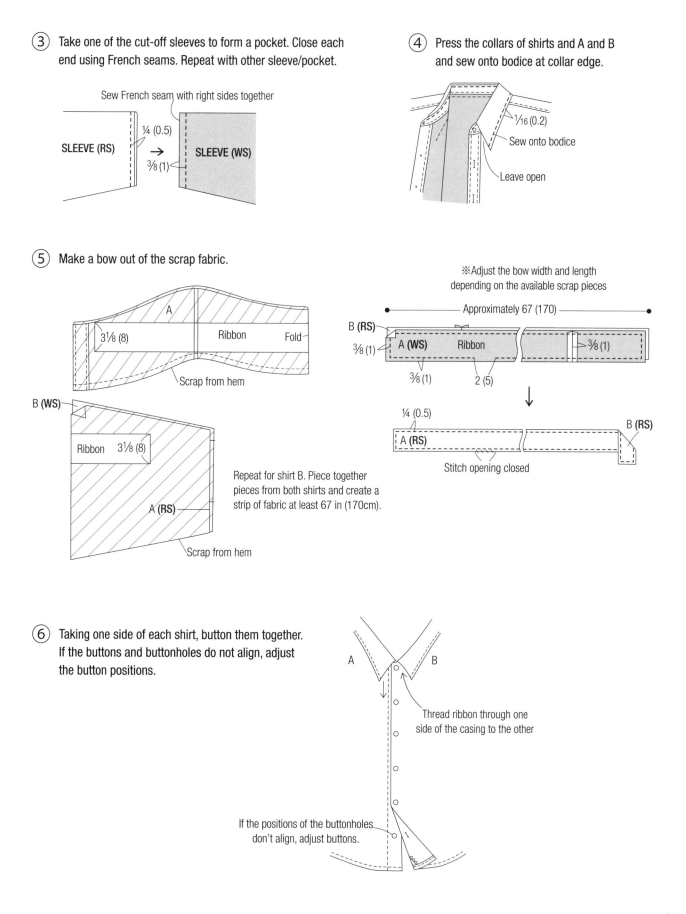

③ **Take one of the cut-off sleeves to form a pocket. Close each end using French seams. Repeat with other sleeve/pocket.**

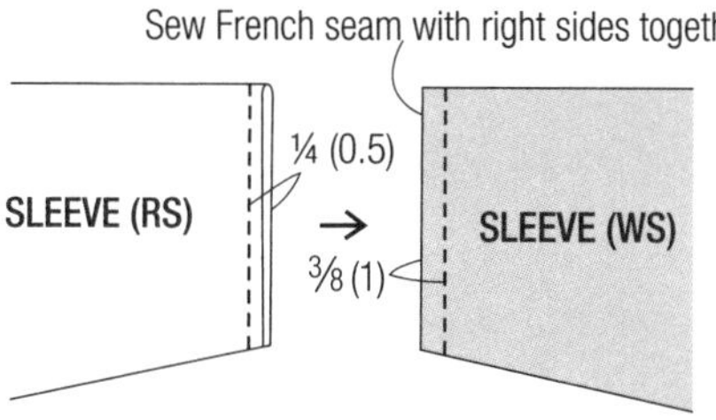
Sew French seam with right sides together
SLEEVE (RS)
¼ (0.5)
⅜ (1)
SLEEVE (WS)

④ **Press the collars of shirts and A and B and sew onto bodice at collar edge.**

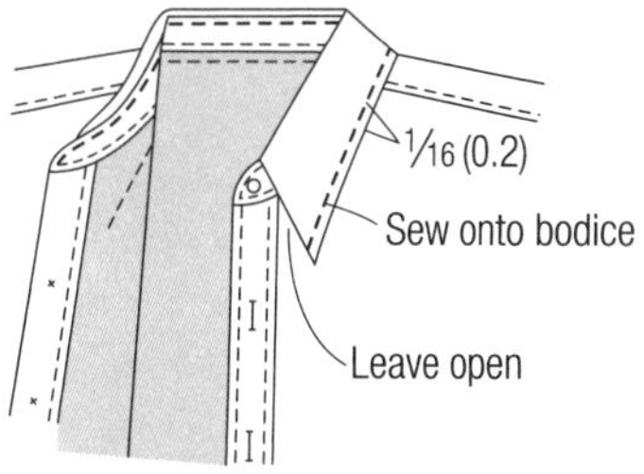
1⁄16 (0.2)
Sew onto bodice
Leave open

⑤ **Make a bow out of the scrap fabric.**

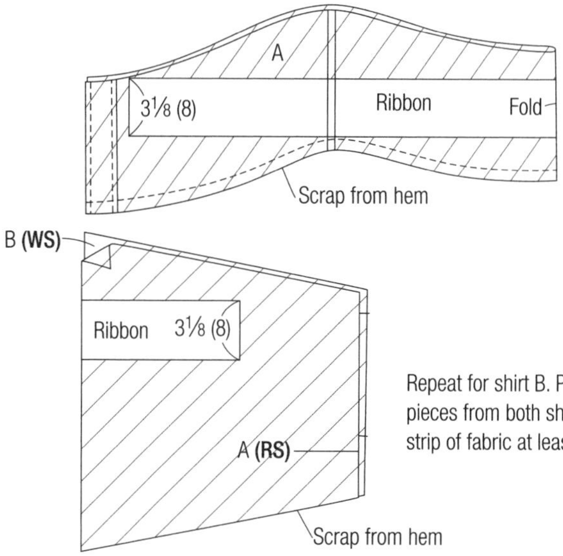
A
3⅛ (8)
Ribbon
Fold
Scrap from hem
B (WS)
Ribbon 3⅛ (8)
A (RS)
Scrap from hem

Repeat for shirt B. Piece together pieces from both shirts and create a strip of fabric at least 67 in (170cm).

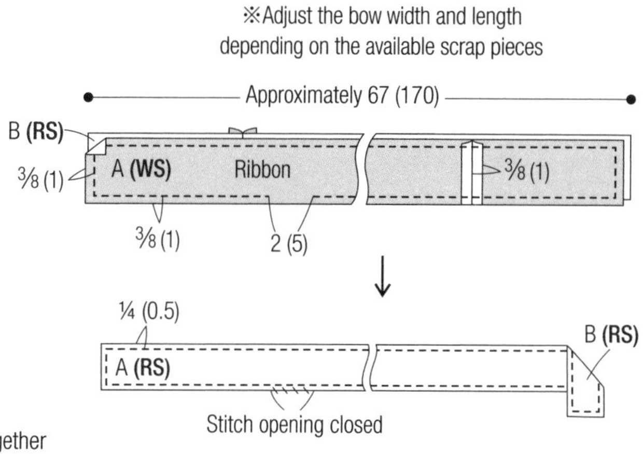
※Adjust the bow width and length depending on the available scrap pieces
Approximately 67 (170)
B (RS)
⅜ (1)
A (WS)
Ribbon
⅜ (1)
⅜ (1)
2 (5)
¼ (0.5)
A (RS)
B (RS)
Stitch opening closed

⑥ **Taking one side of each shirt, button them together. If the buttons and buttonholes do not align, adjust the button positions.**

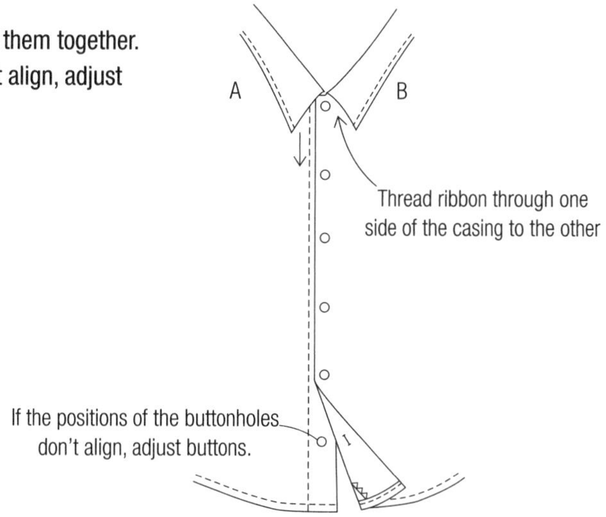
A
B
Thread ribbon through one side of the casing to the other
If the positions of the buttonholes don't align, adjust buttons.

12 Stripes and Liberty Print Dress
▷ page 18

Inspire whimsy by the combining stripes with floral print.
Gather the high waist with a colorful ribbon.

[FINISHED MEASUREMENTS]
(Based on Men's size S)
Length 40⅛ in (102cm)   Bust 37 in (92cm)

＊Measurements are strictly for reference and actual
measurements will depend on original striped T-shirt utilized.

[MATERIALS/SUPPLIES]
Striped T-shirt (three-quarter length sleeve)
Liberty print or floral print fabric (for skirt), 2 yds (1.8m)
    at 45 in (110cm) wide
Ribbon 1⅞ yd (1.7m) at 1 in (2.5cm) wide

＊How to choose a striped T-shirt
A slim fit is recommended.

before

[How to make]

① Shorten the length of the striped T-shirt.

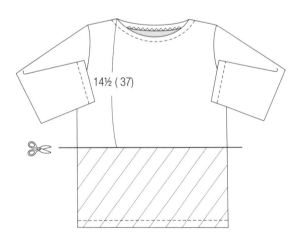

14½ (37)

※Depending on the desired proportions,
 you may want to shorten the sleeves as well.

② Finish the shirt hem and mark
   where the skirt will overlap.

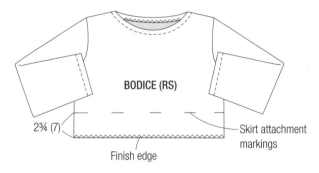

BODICE (RS)

2¾ (7)

Finish edge

Skirt attachment
markings

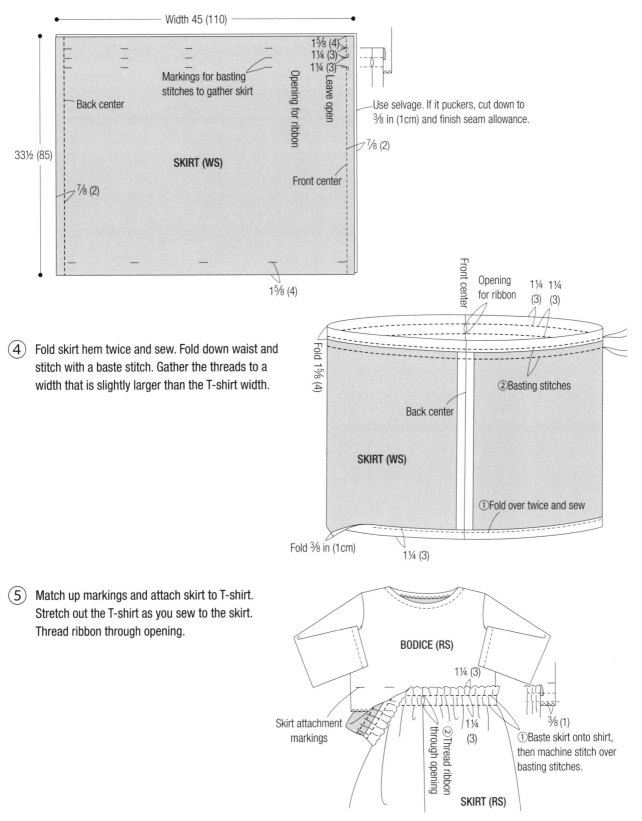

③ For this skirt, the seams will be on the front and back instead of at the sides. With right sides together, sew left and right sides ⅞ in (2cm) from edge, making sure to leave a 1¼ in (3cm) opening near the top of the seam that will be on the front. This is for the threading the ribbon later.

Width 45 (110)

1⅝ (4)
1¼ (3)
1¼ (3)

Markings for basting
stitches to gather skirt

Back center

Opening for ribbon

Leave open

Use selvage. If it puckers, cut down to
⅜ in (1cm) and finish seam allowance.

33½ (85)

⅞ (2)

SKIRT (WS)

Front center

⅞ (2)

1⅝ (4)

④ Fold skirt hem twice and sew. Fold down waist and stitch with a baste stitch. Gather the threads to a width that is slightly larger than the T-shirt width.

Front center

Opening
for ribbon

1¼   1¼
(3)   (3)

Fold 1⅝ (4)

②Basting stitches

Back center

SKIRT (WS)

①Fold over twice and sew

Fold ⅜ in (1cm)

1¼ (3)

⑤ Match up markings and attach skirt to T-shirt. Stretch out the T-shirt as you sew to the skirt. Thread ribbon through opening.

BODICE (RS)

1¼ (3)

Skirt attachment
markings

②Thread ribbon
through opening

1¼
(3)

⅜ (1)

①Baste skirt onto shirt,
then machine stitch over
basting stitches.

SKIRT (RS)

13 Cardigan with Detachable Collar

▷ page 19

Up the chic ante with a rhinestone and pearl-studded detachable peter pan collar worn on top of a striped top. This cardi serves double-duty and can be worn normally or with the opening at the back. For maximum impact, choose large, sparkly gem-like buttons.

[FINISHED MEASUREMENTS]
(Based on Women's size M)
Length 23½ in (60cm)   Bust 36½ in (92cm)

∗ Measurements are strictly for reference and actual measurements will depend on original garments utilized.

[MATERIALS/SUPPLIES]
Striped T-shirt (long-sleeve)
Ribbon (length of T-shirt + ⅞ in [2cm]) x 3 pieces
   (in this case, 2yd [1.8m] total) at 1⅜ in (3.5cm) wide
   (2 for plackets, 1 for facing)
Buttons x 4 at 1 in (2.5cm) diameter
Snaps x 4 sets at ⅝ in (1.5cm) diameter
Fabric for collar 10 in (50cm) at 45 in (110cm) wide
Organza fabric 20 x 12 in (50 × 30cm)
Decorative beads (pearls, rhinestone braids, etc.) as needed
Hook and Eye x 1 set

∗ How to choose a striped T-shirt
For a flattering fit, look for a T-shirt that is neither too loose nor too tight.

before

[How to make]

Cardigan

(1) Measure ⅜ in (1cm) toward the left bodice of the center, and cut vertically down the front of the T-shirt.

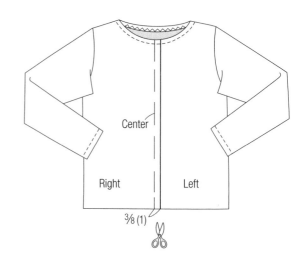

(2) Attach facing to edge of the right bodice opening and attach placket to edge of left bodice opening.

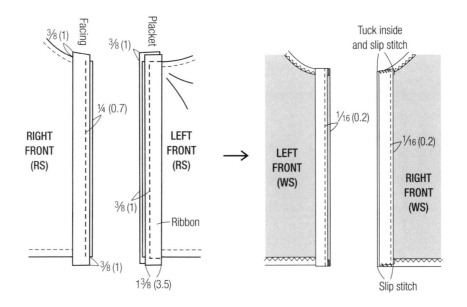

(3) Attach snaps. On the right bodice, sew on decorative buttons.

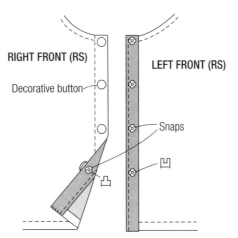

Detachable Collar

① Add seam allowance to the collar pattern. Trace three collars onto fabric. This is to give the collar extra sturdiness with a triple layer.

45 (110) width

••

¼ (0.7)

19¾ (50)

Fold   Fold

¼ (0.7)

¼ (0.7)

¼ (0.7)

② Leaving a 2 in (5cm) opening, sew all three layers together along the shape of the collar.

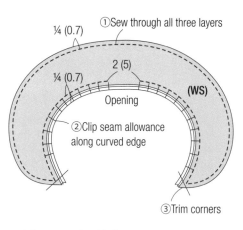

¼ (0.7)   ①Sew through all three layers

¼ (0.7)   2 (5)

Opening   (WS)

②Clip seam allowance along curved edge

③Trim corners

※If you are using thin fabric, iron on interfacing for additional sturdiness.

③ Turn right side out and stitch opening closed. Layer the organza fabric on top of the right side of upper collar and baste.

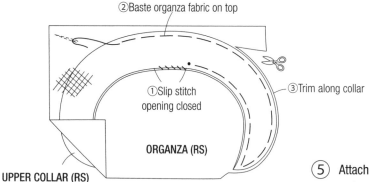

②Baste organza fabric on top

①Slip stitch opening closed

③Trim along collar

ORGANZA (RS)

UPPER COLLAR (RS)

※Note that the upper collar will be composed of two layers (not including the organza) and the undercollar will have only one layer of fabric

④ Attach hook and eye on the undercollar.

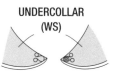

UNDERCOLLAR (WS)

⑤ Attach beads, pearls, etc. on the right side of the upper collar, and sew through the two top layers under the organza to give the embellishment more stability.

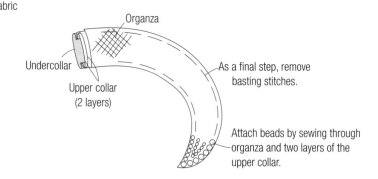

Organza

Undercollar

Upper collar (2 layers)

As a final step, remove basting stitches.

Attach beads by sewing through organza and two layers of the upper collar.

Detachable Collar Pattern Enlarge to 120%

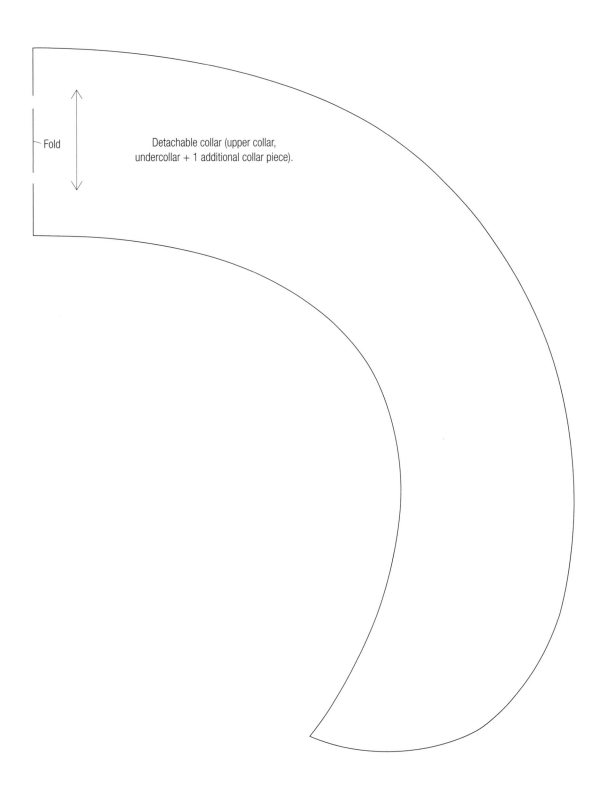

Fold

Detachable collar (upper collar,
undercollar + 1 additional collar piece).

Tunic from an Oversized Scarf

▷ page 20

We bet that you've come across an unforgettable, dynamic scarf that begs to be turned into something more. How about a tunic? Attaching the scarf to a slightly modified T-shirt will transform the look. Bonus: make a handy pouch out of the T-shirt scraps!

[FINISHED MEASUREMENTS]
(Based on Men's size S)
Length 28 in (71cm) Bust 34½ in (88cm)

∗Measurements are strictly for reference and actual measurements will depend on original T-shirt utilized.

[MATERIALS/SUPPLIES]
Striped T-shirt (short sleeves)
Scarf 34 x 34 in (86 × 86cm)

∗How to choose a striped T-shirt and scarf
Opt for a T-shirt that fits like a glove, and the bigger impact the scarf has, the better!

before

[How to make]

① Shorten the T-shirt and cut scarf in half.

12¼ (31)

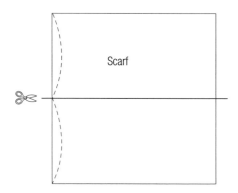

Scarf

② Sew two rows of basting stitches at the top of each scarf half. Sew the sides up to the slit markings.

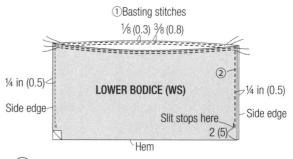

①Basting stitches
⅛ (0.3) ⅜ (0.8)
¼ in (0.5)
Side edge
LOWER BODICE (WS)
②
¼ in (0.5)
Side edge
Slit stops here
2 (5)
Hem

③ Gather the waist so that it is slightly larger than the T-shirt width. With right sides together, stretch out T-shirt waist slightly as you sew the scarf section on.

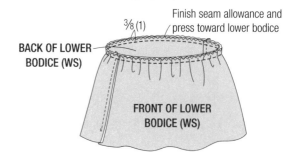

Finish seam allowance and press toward lower bodice
⅜ (1)
BACK OF LOWER BODICE (WS)
FRONT OF LOWER BODICE (WS)

15

Pouch

▷ page 21

Create a handy pouch out of the T-shirt scraps.
You can squeeze out quite a few by varying the
size.

[FINISHED MEASUREMENTS]
11 x 7 in (28 × 18cm)

[MATERIALS/SUPPLIES]
Outer bag (striped T-shirt scraps from pattern
    14) 18 x 9 in (45 × 23cm)
Lining (Rayon) 13 x 9 in (32 × 23cm)
Ruffle fabric (we suggest Liberty print)
    4 in (10cm) at 45 in (110cm) wide
Zipper 10¼ in (26cm)
Ribbon (velour) 4 in (10cm) at 1 in (2.5cm) wide

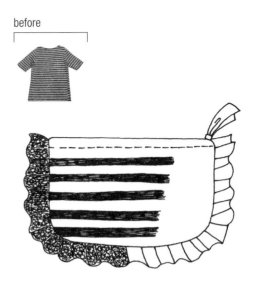

before

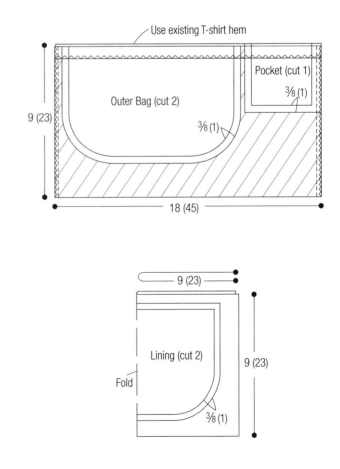

[How to make]

① Trace outer bag pattern piece onto striped T-shirt fabric scrap. Draft
the bag and pocket so that the top is lined up with the pre-existing
finished shirt hem. Add seam allowances to bag and pocket.
Pattern→P.74

Use existing T-shirt hem

Outer Bag (cut 2)

Pocket (cut 1)

⅜ (1)

⅜ (1)

9 (23)

18 (45)

9 (23)

Lining (cut 2)

Fold

9 (23)

⅜ (1)

② Fold fabric for ruffle in half with right sides together, and sew the short end on each side. Turn right side out, press and create gathers by sewing a lengthened running stitch or baste stitch along the raw top edge.

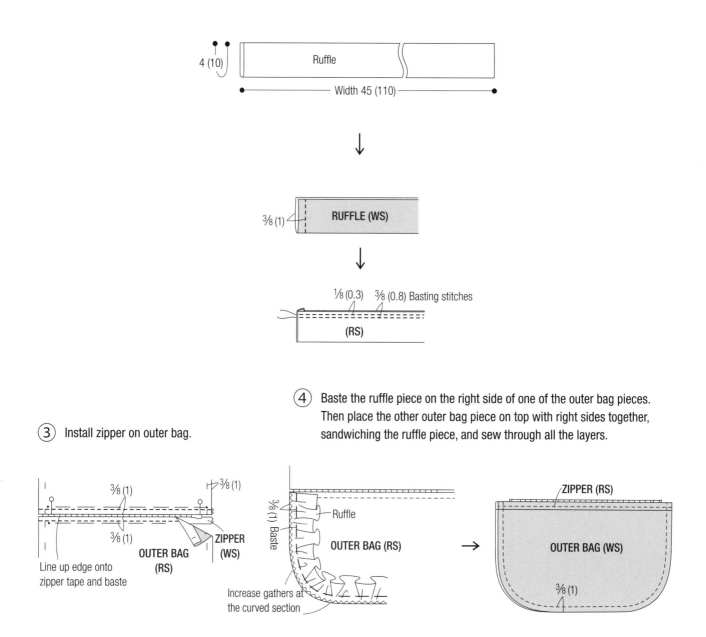

4 (10)

Ruffle

Width 45 (110)

³⁄₈ (1)

RUFFLE (WS)

¹⁄₈ (0.3)   ³⁄₈ (0.8) Basting stitches

(RS)

③ Install zipper on outer bag.

④ Baste the ruffle piece on the right side of one of the outer bag pieces. Then place the other outer bag piece on top with right sides together, sandwiching the ruffle piece, and sew through all the layers.

³⁄₈ (1)   ³⁄₈ (1)

³⁄₈ (1)

ZIPPER (WS)

OUTER BAG (RS)

Line up edge onto zipper tape and baste

³⁄₈ (1) Baste

Ruffle

OUTER BAG (RS)

Increase gathers at the curved section

ZIPPER (RS)

OUTER BAG (WS)

³⁄₈ (1)

⑤ Attach pocket to lining.

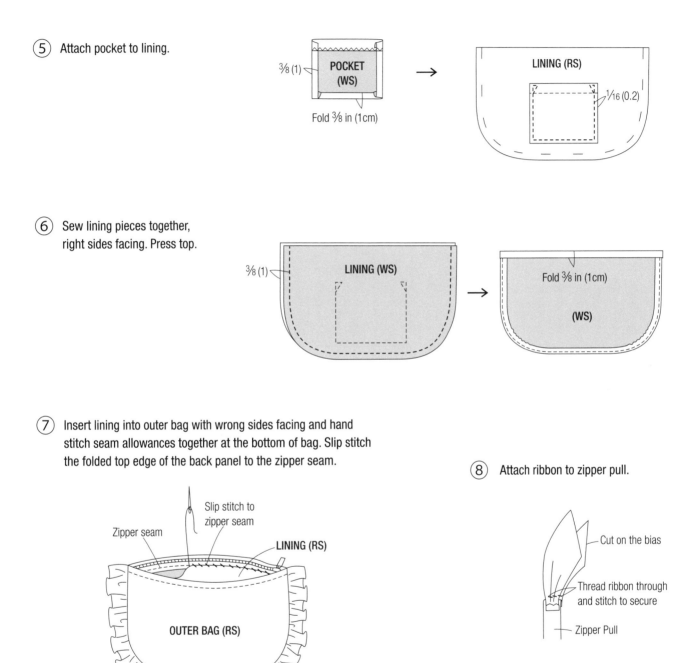

³⁄₈ (1)

POCKET (WS)

Fold ³⁄₈ in (1cm)

→

LINING (RS)

¹⁄₁₆ (0.2)

⑥ Sew lining pieces together, right sides facing. Press top.

³⁄₈ (1)

LINING (WS)

→

Fold ³⁄₈ in (1cm)

(WS)

⑦ Insert lining into outer bag with wrong sides facing and hand stitch seam allowances together at the bottom of bag. Slip stitch the folded top edge of the back panel to the zipper seam.

Slip stitch to zipper seam

Zipper seam

LINING (RS)

OUTER BAG (RS)

⑧ Attach ribbon to zipper pull.

Cut on the bias

Thread ribbon through and stitch to secure

Zipper Pull

Copy Pouch Pattern at 100%

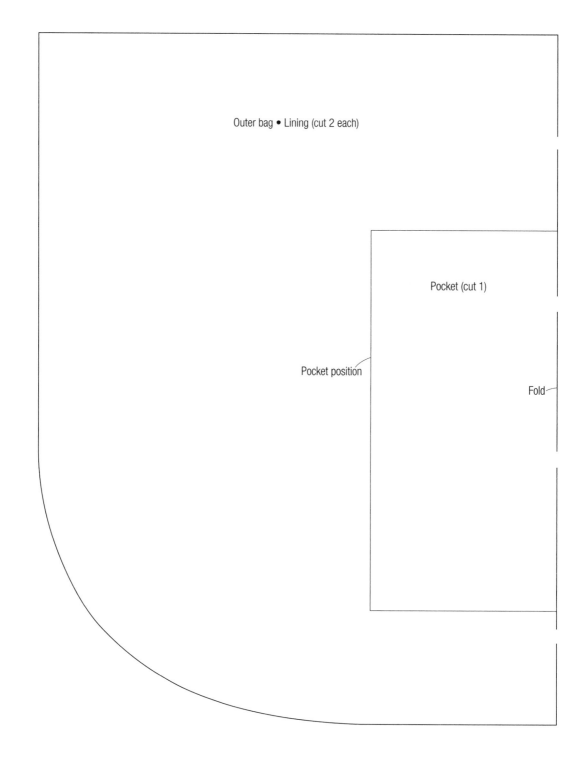

Outer bag • Lining (cut 2 each)

Pocket (cut 1)

Pocket position

Fold

16 Animal Print Collar Top
▷ page 22

Cut the hem on a curve so that it falls just below the navel and alter the sleeves to a puffed, three-quarter length. Then, attach a gathered floaty chiffon collar, and you have a pretty, girly top at the ready!

[FINISHED MEASUREMENTS]
(Based on Men's size XL)
Length 23 in (58cm)   Bust 49 in (124cm)

∗Measurements are strictly for reference and actual measurements will depend on original sweatshirt utilized.

[MATERIALS/SUPPLIES]
Sweatshirt
Chiffon georgette (for collar) 11⅞ in (30cm) at 59 in (150cm) wide

∗How to choose a sweatshirt
We suggest going for a large man's shirt. Because the collar should be the focal point, stick to a shirt with a simple logo.

before

[How to make]

① Cut the sleeves and hem to desired length. Save the ribbed sleeve cuffs.

② Sew basting stitches on sleeve (use illustration as a reference) and gather. The gathered sleeve should fit the circumference of the ribbed sleeve cuff that is slightly stretched. Baste together.

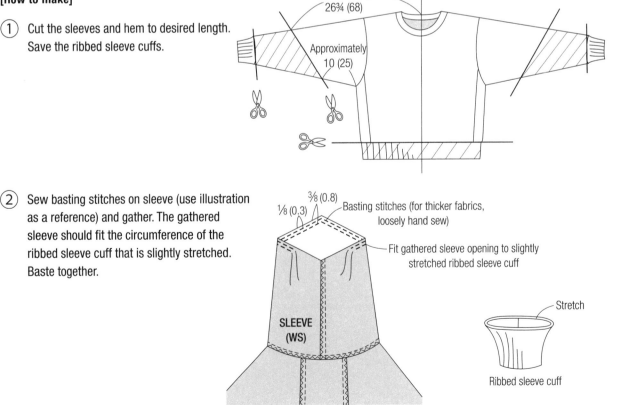

Approximately 26¾ (68)

Approximately 10 (25)

⅜ (0.8)
⅛ (0.3)
Basting stitches (for thicker fabrics, loosely hand sew)

Fit gathered sleeve opening to slightly stretched ribbed sleeve cuff

SLEEVE (WS)

Stretch

Ribbed sleeve cuff

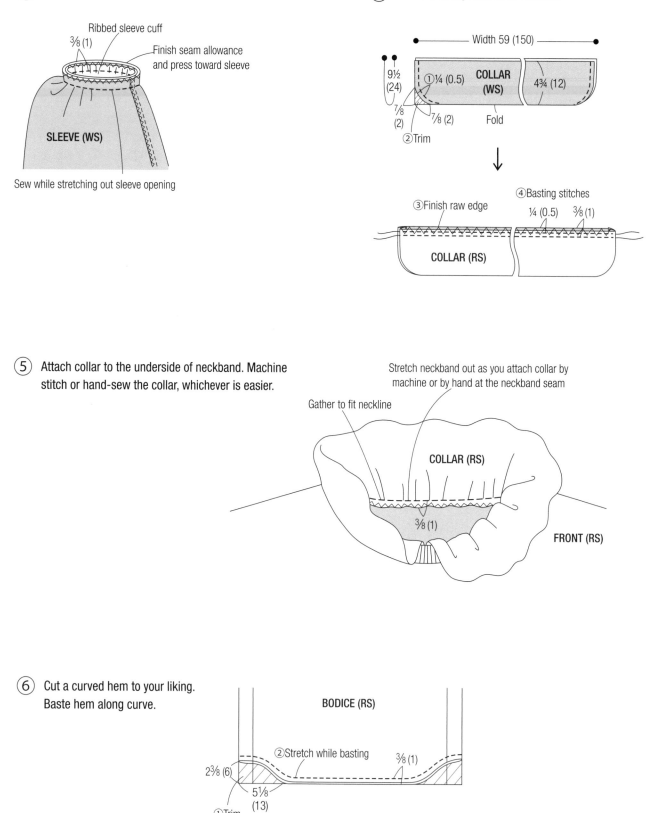

③ Attach ribbed sleeve cuffs.

³⁄₈ (1)
Ribbed sleeve cuff
Finish seam allowance and press toward sleeve

SLEEVE (WS)

Sew while stretching out sleeve opening

④ Make collar, gather to fit neckline.

Width 59 (150)

9½ (24)
①¼ (0.5)
COLLAR (WS)
4¾ (12)
⁷⁄₈ (2)
⁷⁄₈ (2)
Fold
②Trim

③Finish raw edge
④Basting stitches
¼ (0.5)   ³⁄₈ (1)
COLLAR (RS)

⑤ Attach collar to the underside of neckband. Machine stitch or hand-sew the collar, whichever is easier.

Stretch neckband out as you attach collar by machine or by hand at the neckband seam

Gather to fit neckline

COLLAR (RS)

³⁄₈ (1)

FRONT (RS)

⑥ Cut a curved hem to your liking. Baste hem along curve.

BODICE (RS)

②Stretch while basting
³⁄₈ (1)
2³⁄₈ (6)
5¹⁄₈ (13)
①Trim

Tube Top Dress

▷ page 23

The star quality of this garment is the cozy texture and oversized comfort of a much-loved and much-washed sweatshirt. Elastic at the top secures the dress to avoid any mishaps.

[FINISHED MEASUREMENTS]
(Based on Men's size L)
Length 35½ in (90cm)   Bust 34 in (86cm)

∗ Measurements are strictly for reference and actual measurements will depend on original sweatshirt utilized.

[MATERIALS/SUPPLIES]
Sweatshirt
Elastic 28½ in (72cm) at 2 in (5cm) wide (length may vary depending on actual bust measurements

∗ How to choose a sweatshirt
Try to find the largest men's size available to maximize length of the dress.

before

[How to make]

① Cut off sleeves and top of sweatshirt.

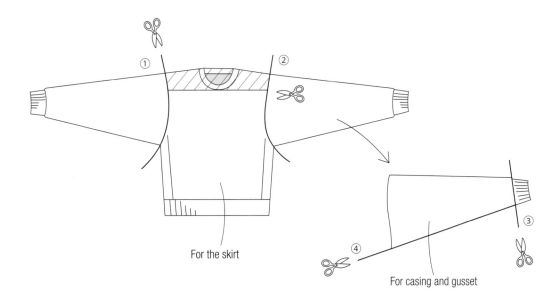

For the skirt

For casing and gusset

(2) Determine the measurements for the casing and gusset on the skirt piece. Draft the casing and gussets from the cut-off sleeve pieces.

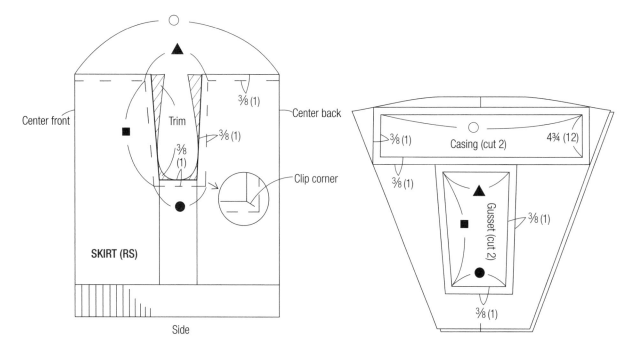

Center front

Trim

⅜ (1)

⅜ (1)

⅜ (1)

Center back

Clip corner

SKIRT (RS)

Side

Casing (cut 2)

⅜ (1)

⅜ (1)

4¾ (12)

Gusset (cut 2)

⅜ (1)

⅜ (1)

(3) Sew skirt and gussets together.

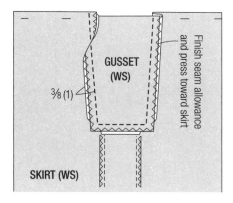

GUSSET (WS)

⅜ (1)

Finish seam allowance and press toward skirt

SKIRT (WS)

(4) Sew casing. Leave an opening for the elastic on one side. Sew the sides and press open.

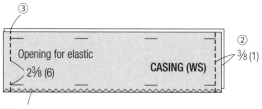

③

Opening for elastic

2⅜ (6)

CASING (WS)

②

⅜ (1)

①Finish raw edges together

(5) Attach casing so that the opening for the elastic is on the left side. Sew skirt and casing with right sides together and open seam allowance.

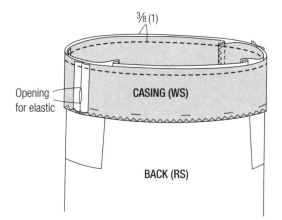

$\frac{3}{8}$ (1)

Opening for elastic

CASING (WS)

BACK (RS)

(6) Fold casing toward wrong side and topstitch.

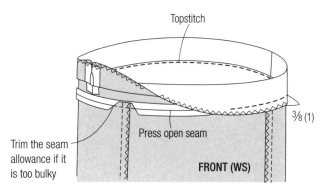

Topstitch

Trim the seam allowance if it is too bulky

Press open seam

$\frac{3}{8}$ (1)

FRONT (WS)

(7) Insert elastic and stitch opening closed. Make sure that the elastic isn't too tight or too loose around the chest before stitching the opening closed.

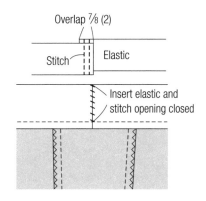

Overlap $\frac{7}{8}$ (2)

Stitch

Elastic

Insert elastic and stitch opening closed

18 Half-and-Half Big Tunic

▷ page 24

Pair a couple of oversized sweatshirts that are about the same size and create a hybrid of logos. Add a feminine touch with the puffed sleeves and A-line silhouette.

[FINISHED MEASUREMENTS]
(Based on Men's size XL)
Length 28½ in (72cm) Bust 57 in (144cm)

∗ Measurements are strictly for reference and actual measurements will depend on original sweatshirt utilized.

[MATERIALS/SUPPLIES]
Sweatshirt (preferably of the same size) x 2

∗ How to choose sweatshirts
Target extra large men's sweatshirts with similar logos/texts.

before

[How to make]

① Place sweatshirts (we'll call them A and B) back-to-back. Determine the A-line dimensions and cut. Also cut one side of the sleeves off.

② Gather sleeves (use illustration as a reference). Fit gathered sleeve opening to slightly stretched ribbed sleeve cuff and baste.

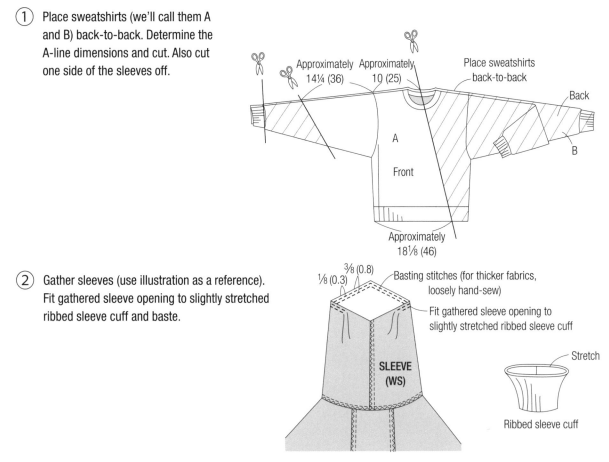

Approximately 14¼ (36)   Approximately 10 (25)

Place sweatshirts back-to-back

Back

A
Front

B

Approximately 18⅛ (46)

⅜ (0.8)   ⅛ (0.3)   Basting stitches (for thicker fabrics, loosely hand-sew)

Fit gathered sleeve opening to slightly stretched ribbed sleeve cuff

SLEEVE (WS)

Stretch

Ribbed sleeve cuff

③ Attach ribbed sleeve cuffs.

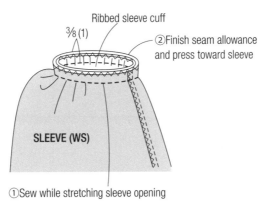

Ribbed sleeve cuff

⅜ (1)

②Finish seam allowance and press toward sleeve

SLEEVE (WS)

①Sew while stretching sleeve opening

④ Finish the front center seams of sweatshirts A and B separately. With right sides together, align the two sweatshirts and cut hem to the shorter length. Baste hem. Sew center seam up to the slit marking. Press open seam allowance.

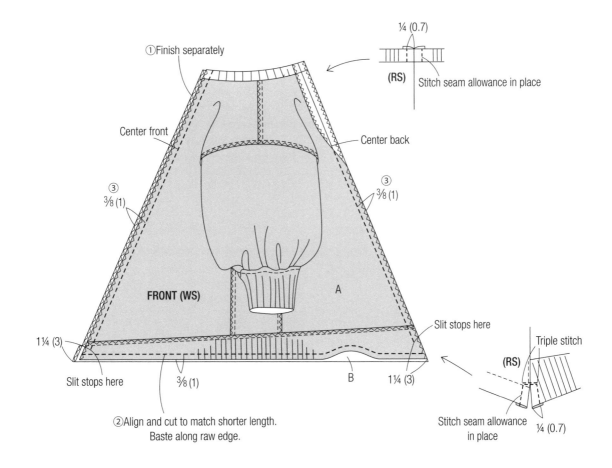

①Finish separately

¼ (0.7)

(RS) Stitch seam allowance in place

Center front

Center back

③
⅜ (1)

③
⅜ (1)

FRONT (WS)

A

Slit stops here

1¼ (3)

Triple stitch

(RS)

Slit stops here

⅜ (1)

B

1¼ (3)

②Align and cut to match shorter length. Baste along raw edge.

Stitch seam allowance in place

¼ (0.7)

19 Hoodie Dress

▷ page 25

Upcycle a thrift store lace skirt and hoodie into a whole new outfit. Add extra sweetness with three-quarter puffed sleeves and replace the hood drawstring with a dainty lace ribbon.

[FINISHED MEASUREMENTS]
(Based on Men's size M)
Length 44½ in (113cm)   Bust 38 in (96cm)

∗ Measurements are strictly for reference and actual measurements will depend on original garments utilized.

[MATERIALS/SUPPLIES]
Hoodie
Long skirt (use a tiered lace skirt with a lining if possible)
Lace ribbon 1¼ yd (1.1m) at ⅞ in (2cm) wide

∗ How to choose a hoodie
Avoid hoodies that are too generous in size to preserve a balanced proportion between the top and skirt.

before

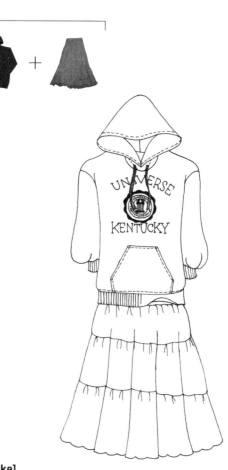

[How to make]

① Cut hoodie sleeves and skirt to desired length.
    Save the ribbed sleeve cuffs.

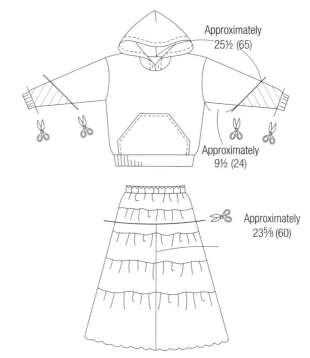

Approximately 25½ (65)

Approximately 9½ (24)

Approximately 23⅝ (60)

② Gather sleeves (use illustration for reference). Fit gathered sleeve opening to slightly stretched ribbed sleeve cuff and baste.

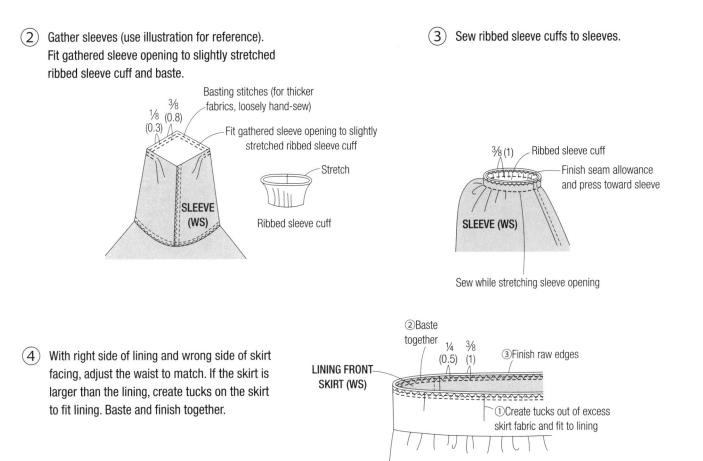

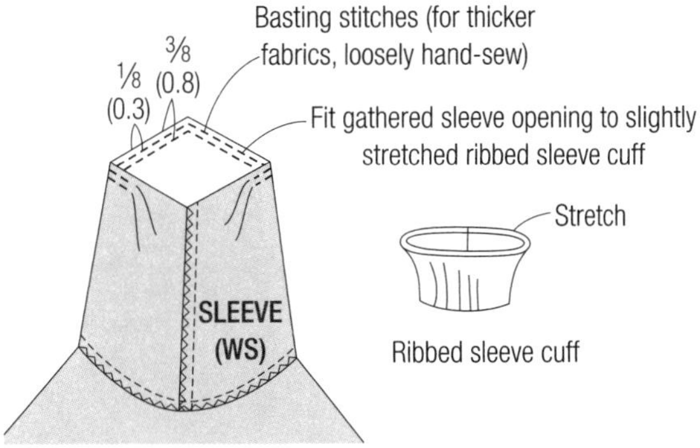
Basting stitches (for thicker fabrics, loosely hand-sew)
⅛ (0.3)
⅜ (0.8)
Fit gathered sleeve opening to slightly stretched ribbed sleeve cuff
Stretch
SLEEVE (WS)
Ribbed sleeve cuff

③ Sew ribbed sleeve cuffs to sleeves.

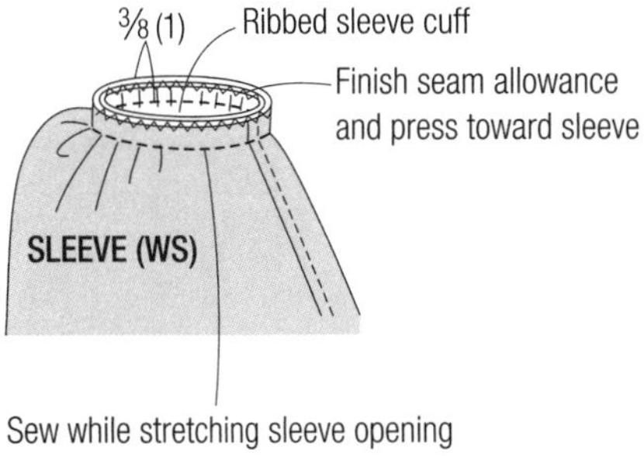
⅜ (1)
Ribbed sleeve cuff
Finish seam allowance and press toward sleeve
SLEEVE (WS)
Sew while stretching sleeve opening

④ With right side of lining and wrong side of skirt facing, adjust the waist to match. If the skirt is larger than the lining, create tucks on the skirt to fit lining. Baste and finish together.

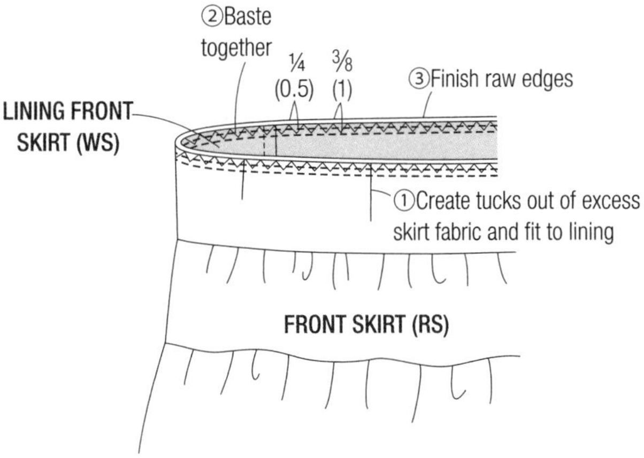
②Baste together
¼ (0.5)
⅜ (1)
③Finish raw edges
LINING FRONT SKIRT (WS)
①Create tucks out of excess skirt fabric and fit to lining
FRONT SKIRT (RS)

⑤ Baste skirt to hoodie, then topstitch.

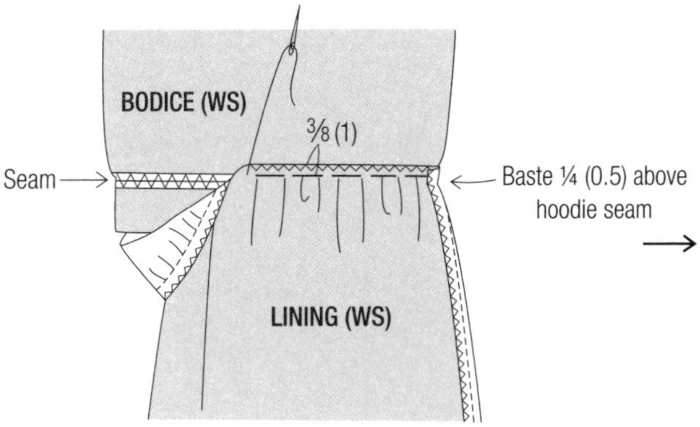
BODICE (WS)
⅜ (1)
Seam
Baste ¼ (0.5) above hoodie seam
LINING (WS)

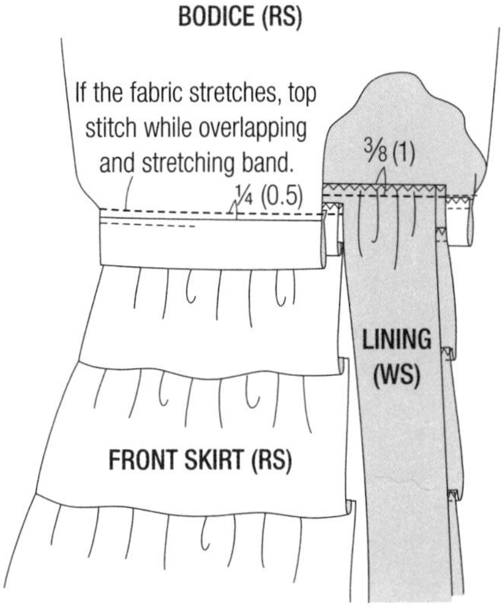
BODICE (RS)
If the fabric stretches, top stitch while overlapping and stretching band.
¼ (0.5)
⅜ (1)
LINING (WS)
FRONT SKIRT (RS)

⑥ Thread lace ribbon through hood casing.

20 Coat with Scarf Collar and Details

▷ page 27

Take a stand-up collar coat and add some pizzazz with a gathered collar made out of a scarf. You can also casually embellish the coat by appliquéing sections of the scarf remnants.

[FINISHED MEASUREMENTS]
(Based on Women's size M)
Length 30¾ in (78cm)   Bust 37 in (94cm)

∗ Measurements are strictly for reference and actual measurements will depend on original coat utilized.

[MATERIALS/SUPPLIES]
Stand-up collar coat
Scarf (for collar and appliqué) 26 x 26 in (66 × 66cm)
Fusible interfacing (for appliqué) as needed

∗ How to choose a coat
Select a coat in your size.

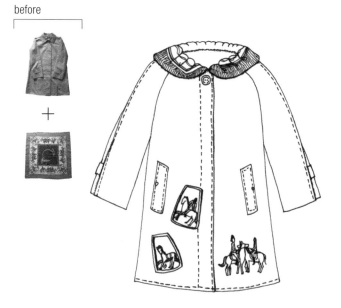

before

+

[How to make]

① Cut off the existing collar and shorten the coat to desired length.

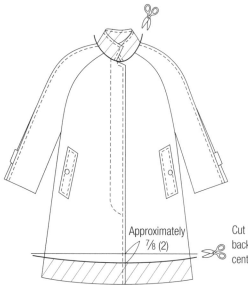

Approximately ⅞ (2)

Cut hem for both front and back, gently curving toward center to desired length.

② Draft collar from scarf.

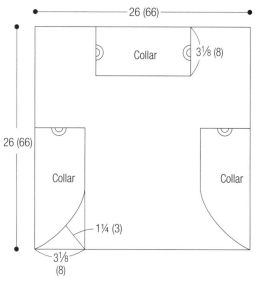

26 (66)

26 (66)

Collar — 3⅛ (8)

Collar

Collar

1¼ (3)

3⅛ (8)

※ Outer collar dimensions = neckline measurement x 2 (approximately). Take into consideration the design/print elements when cutting the collar and try to match prints where possible. For any remaining scarf sections that you want to use as appliqué, add a ¼ in (0.5cm) seam allowance and cut.

③ Baste lining to coat at neckline and hem.

④ Assemble collar pieces using French seams (press seam allowance toward center). Finish curved raw edge of collar and gather to fit neckline.

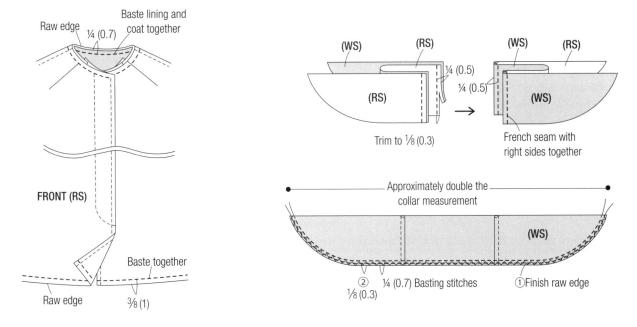

⑤ Place right side of collar on wrong side of coat neckline and sew.

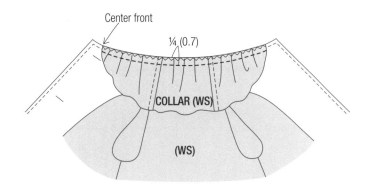

⑥ Appliqué scarf pieces as desired.

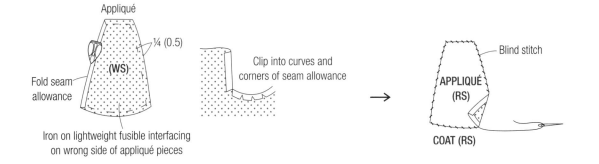

21 Scarf Motif Charms

▷ page 28

If a particularly unique design element catches your eye, cut it out from the scarf, fill it with stuffing, and voila: a charm! Give it extra sparkle with a few well-placed rhinestones, and attach to a bag or keychain.

[MATERIALS/SUPPLIES]
Scarf
Synthetic stuffing as needed
Ribbon 1½ in (4cm) at ¼ in (0.5cm) wide

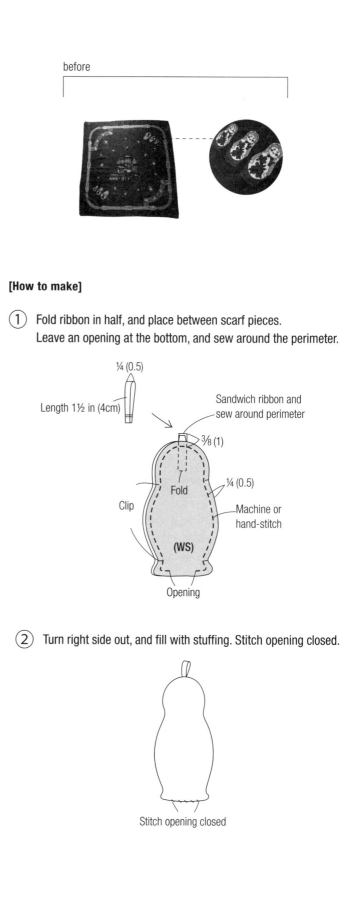

before

[How to make]

① Fold ribbon in half, and place between scarf pieces.
Leave an opening at the bottom, and sew around the perimeter.

¼ (0.5)

Length 1½ in (4cm)

Sandwich ribbon and sew around perimeter

⅜ (1)

Fold

¼ (0.5)

Clip

Machine or hand-stitch

(WS)

Opening

② Turn right side out, and fill with stuffing. Stitch opening closed.

Stitch opening closed

22 Trench Coat Poncho

▷ page 29

Transform a no-nonsense men's double-breasted trench coat into a playful poncho by chopping off the sleeves. Hand-stitch appliqués cut from a bold and colorful scarf for added visual interest.

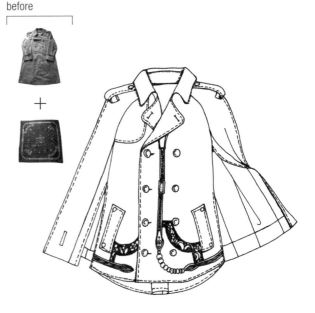

before

+

[FINISHED MEASUREMENTS]
(Based on Men's size L)
Length 30 in (76cm)   Bust 41 in (104cm)

＊Measurements are strictly for reference and actual measurements will depend on original coat utilized.

[MATERIALS/SUPPLIES]
Trench coat
Scarf (for appliqué) 36 x 36 in (90 × 90cm)
Lightweight fusible interfacing (for appliqué) as needed

＊How to choose a trench coat and scarf
Seek out a large men's size for the coat. For the scarf we recommend bold prints like the chain pattern on the model.

[PREPARATION]
Iron lightweight fusible interfacing onto entire scarf.

[How to make]

① Cut the coat to desired length. Cut sides and along the underarms or sleeves.

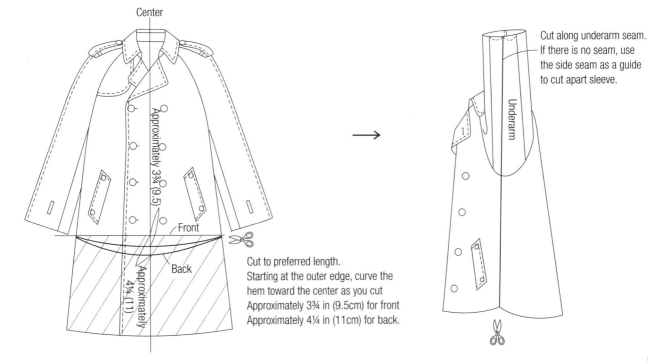

Center

Approximately 3¾ (9.5)

Front

Back

Approximately 4¼ (11)

Cut to preferred length.
Starting at the outer edge, curve the hem toward the center as you cut
Approximately 3¾ in (9.5cm) for front
Approximately 4¼ in (11cm) for back.

Cut along underarm seam.
If there is no seam, use the side seam as a guide to cut apart sleeve.

Underarm

② Open the sleeve and side and baste lining to outer fabric to prevent shifting. Finish lining and outer fabric together on each cut edge. For the hem, baste lining and outer fabrics together.

③ For the underarm and side edges on the front side of the coat, fold the edge toward the wrong side and sew.

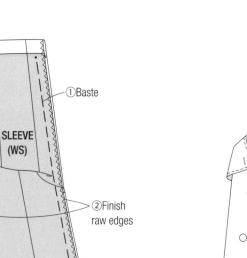

①Baste

SLEEVE (WS)

FRONT (RS)

②Finish raw edges

BACK (WS)

Raw edge

³⁄₈ (1)

③Baste

Front side

³⁄₈ (0.8)

Fold ³⁄₈ (1)

④ Sew the underarm and side edges on the backside together, right sides facing (press seam allowance toward back).

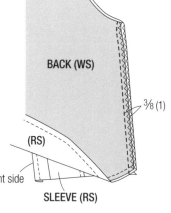

BACK (WS)

³⁄₈ (1)

(RS)

Front side

SLEEVE (RS)

⑤ Add seam allowance to scarf elements that will become appliqués and cut out. Position the appliqués on coat and blind stitch.

23 Patchwork Dress
▷ page 30

Square bandannas are plentiful at dollar and thrift stores, and what better way to repurpose them than to stitch them together into a simple dress? If possible, collect several bandannas in the same general color family even if they are not identical in hue. Tying the corners of the hem will allow the dress to swing jauntily as you walk.

[FINISHED MEASUREMENTS]
Length 38 in (96cm)   Bust 49½ in (126cm)

[MATERIALS/SUPPLIES]
Bandannas x 8, 20½ x 20½ in (52 × 52cm)

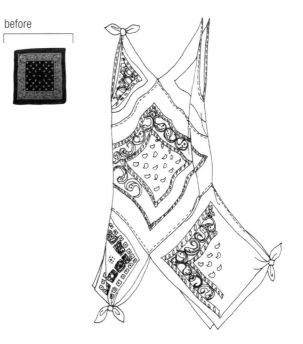

before

[How to make]

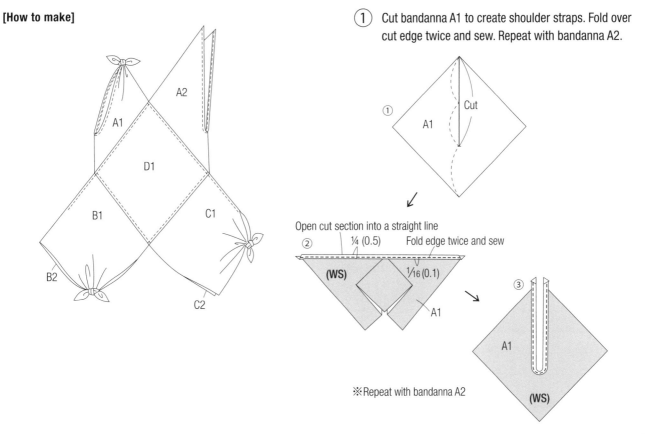

① Cut bandanna A1 to create shoulder straps. Fold over cut edge twice and sew. Repeat with bandanna A2.

① A1   Cut

Open cut section into a straight line
② ¼ (0.5)   Fold edge twice and sew
(WS)   1⁄16 (0.1)   A1

③ A1   (WS)

※Repeat with bandanna A2

② Place bandanna B on top with a ¼ (0.5) overlap and sew up to marking.

③ Place bandanna D on top of bandannas B and C with a ¼ (0.5) overlap and sew.

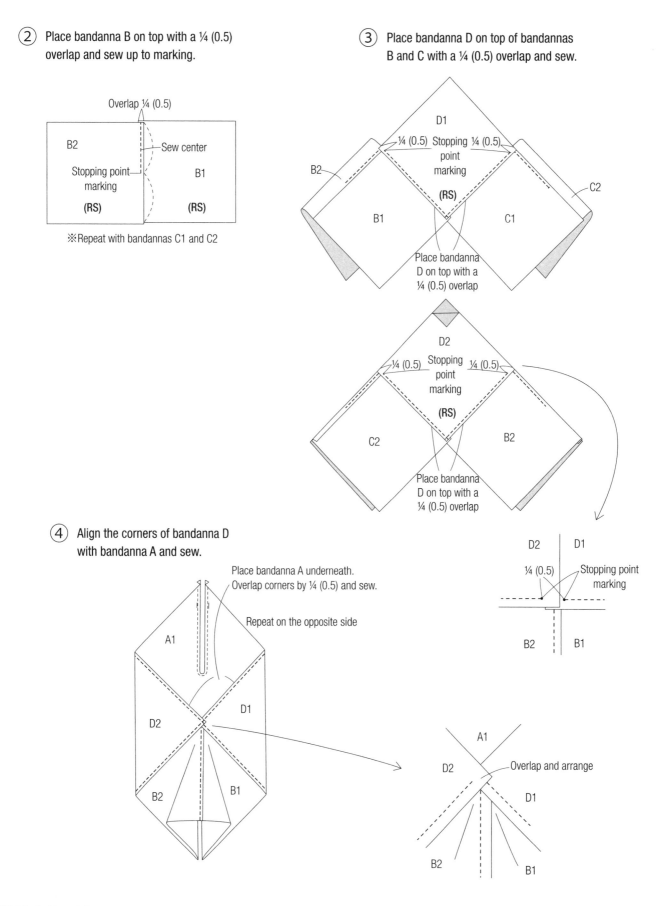

Overlap ¼ (0.5)

B2

Sew center

Stopping point marking

(RS)

B1

(RS)

※Repeat with bandannas C1 and C2

D1

¼ (0.5) Stopping point marking ¼ (0.5)

B2

(RS)

B1

C1

C2

Place bandanna D on top with a ¼ (0.5) overlap

D2

¼ (0.5) Stopping point marking ¼ (0.5)

(RS)

C2

B2

Place bandanna D on top with a ¼ (0.5) overlap

④ Align the corners of bandanna D with bandanna A and sew.

Place bandanna A underneath. Overlap corners by ¼ (0.5) and sew.

Repeat on the opposite side

A1

D2

D1

B2

B1

D2

D1

¼ (0.5)

Stopping point marking

B2

B1

A1

D2

Overlap and arrange

D1

B2

B1

24 Child's Camisole and Skirt

▷ page 31

Another great way to upcycle bandannas is to sew them into a pint-sized ruffled camisole and flouncy skirt. Rather than brand new bandannas, use ones that have a soft and supple feel, ideal for kids.

[FINISHED MEASUREMENTS]
For child 31½–35½ in (80~90cm) tall
•Camisole
Length 8 in (20cm)   Bust 16½ in (42cm)
 •Skirt
Length 7½ in (19cm)   Waist 12½ in (32cm)

[MATERIALS/SUPPLIES]
•Camisole
Bandanna 20½ x 20½ in (52 × 52cm)
Elastic ¼ in (6mm) wide, 8 in (20cm) long
•Skirt
Bandanna x 2, 20½ x 20½ in (52 × 52cm)
Elastic ¼ in (6mm) wide, 15¾ in (40cm) long

before

[How to make]

Camisole

① Use the edge for hem. Adjust neck tie based on available fabric.

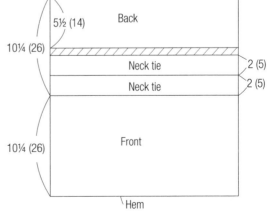

② Fold edge of ruffle twice toward the right side and sew.

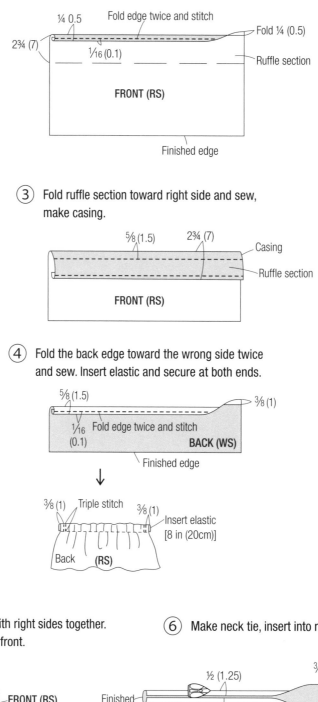

¼ 0.5   Fold edge twice and stitch

2¾ (7)

Fold ¼ (0.5)

¹⁄₁₆ (0.1)

Ruffle section

FRONT (RS)

Finished edge

③ Fold ruffle section toward right side and sew, make casing.

⅝ (1.5)   2¾ (7)

Casing

Ruffle section

FRONT (RS)

④ Fold the back edge toward the wrong side twice and sew. Insert elastic and secure at both ends.

⅝ (1.5)

³⁄₈ (1)

¹⁄₁₆ (0.1)   Fold edge twice and stitch

BACK (WS)

Finished edge

³⁄₈ (1)   Triple stitch   ³⁄₈ (1)

Insert elastic
[8 in (20cm)]

Back   (RS)

⑤ Sew front and back at sides with right sides together. Press seam allowance toward front.

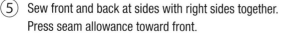

FRONT (RS)

³⁄₈ (1)

BACK (WS)   Finished edge

⑥ Make neck tie, insert into ruffle casing.

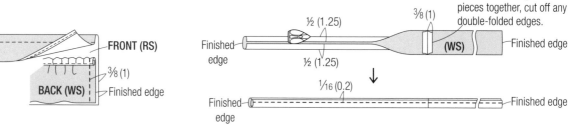

When assembling the tie pieces together, cut off any double-folded edges.

½ (1.25)

³⁄₈ (1)

Finished edge

½ (1.25)

(WS)

Finished edge

¹⁄₁₆ (0.2)

Finished edge

Finished edge

Skirt

① Cut bandanna in half for skirt.
Use the printed section for the drawstring.

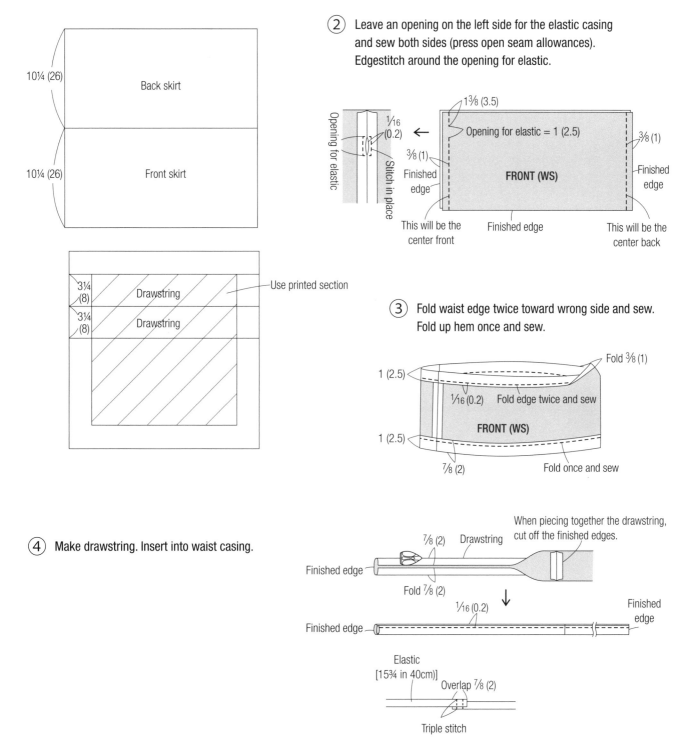

10¼ (26) Back skirt

10¼ (26) Front skirt

3¼ (8) Drawstring

3¼ (8) Drawstring

Use printed section

② Leave an opening on the left side for the elastic casing
and sew both sides (press open seam allowances).
Edgestitch around the opening for elastic.

1⅜ (3.5)

Opening for elastic

1/16 (0.2)

Stitch in place

Opening for elastic = 1 (2.5)

3/8 (1)

3/8 (1)

FRONT (WS)

Finished edge

Finished edge

This will be the center front

Finished edge

This will be the center back

③ Fold waist edge twice toward wrong side and sew.
Fold up hem once and sew.

Fold 3/8 (1)

1 (2.5)

1/16 (0.2) Fold edge twice and sew

FRONT (WS)

1 (2.5)

7/8 (2)

Fold once and sew

④ Make drawstring. Insert into waist casing.

When piecing together the drawstring,
cut off the finished edges.

7/8 (2) Drawstring

Finished edge

Fold 7/8 (2)

1/16 (0.2)

Finished edge

Finished edge

Elastic
[15¾ in 40cm)]

Overlap 7/8 (2)

Triple stitch

25 Drawstring Purse
▷ page 32

The angled ruffle is especially charming for this drawstring type purse. Can be used by both girls and women.

[FINISHED MEASUREMENTS]
8 x 10 in (20 × 25cm) (The pouch portion)

[MATERIALS/SUPPLIES]
Bandanna x 3, 20½ x 20½ in (52 × 52cm)

before

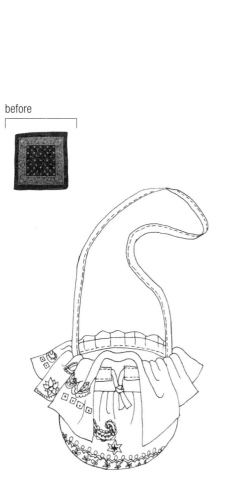

[How to make]

① For the shoulder strap, cut off the two finished edges of bandanna A. Cut out a square from the center of bandanna B. Baste two rows all around the perimeter of bandanna C.

A shoulder strap, drawstring.

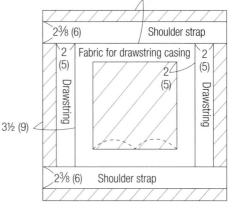

3½ (9)

2⅜ (6) Shoulder strap

2 (5) Fabric for drawstring casing 2 (5)

2 (5)

Drawstring

3½ (9)

Drawstring

2⅜ (6) Shoulder strap

B Ruffle

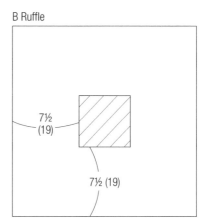

7½ (19)

7½ (19)

C Pouch

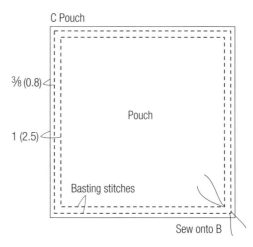

⅜ (0.8)

1 (2.5)

Pouch

Basting stitches

Sew onto B

② Fold seam allowance for drawstring casing and attach to B.

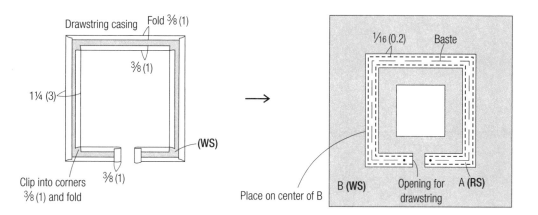

Drawstring casing
Fold ⅜ (1)
⅜ (1)
1¼ (3)
(WS)
Clip into corners
⅜ (1) and fold
⅜ (1)

Place on center of B

1/16 (0.2)
Baste
B (WS)
Opening for drawstring
A (RS)

③ Fit gathered C to B at the opening corners and sew.

Clip into corners
⅜ (1)
Match corners of B and C
C (WS)
B (WS)

French seam ⅝ in (1.5cm)
Shoulder strap position
C (RS)
B (RS)

④ Make and attach shoulder strap.
Make drawstring and thread through opening.

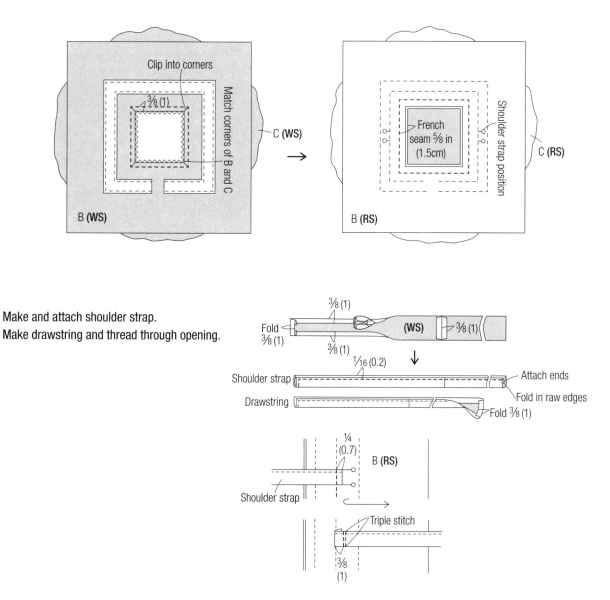

⅜ (1)
Fold ⅜ (1)
⅜ (1)
(WS)
⅜ (1)

1/16 (0.2)
Shoulder strap
Drawstring
Attach ends
Fold in raw edges
Fold ⅜ (1)

¼ (0.7)
B (RS)
Shoulder strap
Triple stitch
⅜ (1)

Published in 2015 by Tuttle Publishing, an imprint of Periplus Editions (HK) Ltd.

www.tuttlepublishing.com

ISBN 978-4-8053-1365-7

VINTAGE REMAKE: BOYS FURUGI WO GIRLS ITEM NI REMAKE
by Violette Room
© 2012 Violette Room
English Translation © 2015 Periplus Editions (HK) Ltd.
English translation rights arranged with
EDUCATIONAL FOUNDATION BUNKA GAKUEN BUNKA PUBLISHING BUREAU
through Japan UNI Agency, Inc. Tokyo
Translated from Japanese by Sanae Ishida
All rights reserved.

Original Japanese edition
Publisher: Sunao Onuma
Book design by Makiko Kimura
Photography by Eri Takahashi
Styling by Miyuki Kato
Hair and Make-up by Yumiko Chuugun
Sewing Assistant Masako Ueki
Instructions editor Mutsuko Sukegawa
Tracing by Toshio Usui
Illustrations Akiko Sasaki
Proofreading by Masako Mukai
Editing by Kaori Tanaka (Bunka Publishing Bureau)

Distributed by

North America, Latin America & Europe
Tuttle Publishing, 364 Innovation Drive,
North Clarendon, VT 05759-9436 U.S.A.
Tel: 1 (802) 773-8930; Fax: 1 (802) 773-6993
info@tuttlepublishing.com; www.tuttlepublishing.com

Japan
Tuttle Publishing, Yaekari Building, 3rd Floor, 5-4-12 Osaki,
Shinagawa-ku, Tokyo 141 0032
Tel: (81) 3 5437-0171; Fax: (81) 3 5437-0755
sales@tuttle.co.jp; www.tuttle.co.jp

Asia Pacific
Berkeley Books Pte. Ltd.
61 Tai Seng Avenue #02-12, Singapore 534167
Tel: (65) 6280-1330; Fax: (65) 6280-6290
inquiries@periplus.com.sg; www.periplus.com

Printed in Malaysia   1504TW
18 17 16 15   6 5 4 3 2 1

The Tuttle Story
"Books to Span the East and West"

Many people are surprised to learn that the world's largest publisher of books on Asia had its humble beginnings in the tiny American state of Vermont. The company's founder, Charles E. Tuttle, belonged to a New England family steeped in publishing.

Tuttle's father was a noted antiquarian dealer in Rutland, Vermont. Young Charles honed his knowledge of the trade working in the family bookstore, and later in the rare books section of Columbia University Library. His passion for beautiful books—old and new—never wavered throughout his long career as a bookseller and publisher.

After graduating from Harvard, Tuttle enlisted in the military and in 1945 was sent to Tokyo to work on General Douglas MacArthur's staff. He was tasked with helping to revive the Japanese publishing industry, which had been utterly devastated by the war. When his tour of duty was completed, he left the military, married a talented and beautiful singer, Reiko Chiba, and in 1948 began several successful business ventures.

To his astonishment, Tuttle discovered that postwar Tokyo was actually a book-lover's paradise. He befriended dealers in the Kanda district and began supplying rare Japanese editions to American libraries. He also imported American books to sell to the thousands of GIs stationed in Japan. By 1949, Tuttle's business was thriving, and he opened Tokyo's very first English-language bookstore in the Takashimaya Department Store in Ginza, to great success. Two years later, he began publishing books to fulfill the growing interest of foreigners in all things Asian.

Though a westerner, Tuttle was hugely instrumental in bringing a knowledge of Japan and Asia to a world hungry for information about the East. By the time of his death in 1993, he had published over 6,000 books on Asian culture, history and art—a legacy honored by Emperor Hirohito in 1983 with the "Order of the Sacred Treasure," the highest honor Japan can bestow upon a non-Japanese.

The Tuttle company today maintains an active backlist of some 1,500 titles, many of which have been continuously in print since the 1950s and 1960s—a great testament to Charles Tuttle's skill as a publisher. More than 60 years after its founding, Tuttle Publishing is more active today than at any time in its history, still inspired by Charles Tuttle's core mission—to publish fine books to span the East and West and provide a greater understanding of each.